1400

Pebble Hill

The Story of a Plantation

PEBBLE HILL:
THE STORY OF A PLANTATION

by

WILLIAM WARREN ROGERS

SENTRY PRESS

Tallahassee, Florida

1979

Printed and Bound in the United States

of America by Sentry Press

Tallahassee, Florida

This book is jointly dedicated
to Thomas Jefferson Johnson and
to Elisabeth Ireland Poe

TABLE OF CONTENTS

ILLUSTRATIONS

MAPS AND TABLES

While the earth remaineth, seedtime and harvest, and cold and heat, and summer and winter, and day and night shall not cease.
Genesis 8:22

PREFACE

The history of Pebble Hill plantation and that of Thomas County is inseparable. Located in the Southwest region of Georgia, the plantation began with Thomas County and has enjoyed a remarkable continuity down to the present. Until the last years of the nineteenth century the record of Pebble Hill and the people who lived there reveal much about agrarian life in the rest of Georgia. After that, the plantation was anything but typical. It is with the hope of presenting a permanent and accurate (to the extent that accuracy can prevail over unintentional but inevitable errors) historical account that this work has been undertaken. The book has been sponsored by the Thomas County Historical Society. Earlier, the Society supported the preparation and publication of three works on the history of Thomas County.

Basic to my writing was the research material located in the Thomas County Courthouse at Thomasville. Offering helpful advice and rectifying false starts were the Clerk of the Circuit Court, the late William A. Watt, Jr., and the current Clerk, Ann Maddox, as well as their staffs, and the staff in the office of the Judge of Probate. I also appreciate the aid received from the personnel at other locales in Georgia. Those included employees and officials at the Decatur County Courthouse, Bainbridge; the Grady County Courthouse, Cairo; the Pulaski County Courthouse, Hawkinsville; and the Early County Courthouse, Blakely.

At the Cairo Public Library I received courteous assistance, and at the Thomasville Public Library I owe a debt to Mrs. Jeannette Singletary, Mrs. Meg Richards, Mrs. Elise Whitehead, Mrs. Vivian Melton, and the late Mrs. Elvera Johnson. Another Thomasville librarian, Mary Harris, read the manuscript, made numerous insightful suggestions, and went out of her way to furnish assistance. I wish also to thank Mrs. Maybell Elliott, a generous person, good friend, and authority on Pebble Hill; Mrs. Marguerite Williams, who permitted the use of her historical files; Norman C. Larson, former Director of Thomasville Landmarks, Inc.; Charles T. Hill, Curator of the Thomas County Historical Society Museum and widely knowledgeable about Thomas County history; the late Mrs. William A. Watt, Sr.; the late Fred Scott, Jr.; Mary Scott; John Hebron Moore; William Brueckheimer; James P. Jones; Mrs. Martha Mitchell; Mrs. Polly Singletary; Mrs. Neil Boland; Mrs. Thelma Lawyer; Mrs. Alice Massey; Leroy Edwards; Mrs. Gertrude Britton; and Livingston Ireland. Particularly helpful were Parker Poe and Michael Singletary. I am indebted to Louise Humphrey, Kate Ireland, and Robert Livingston Ireland, III, for reading the manuscript and providing me with information about the Hanna family.

Mrs. May A. Walton of Augusta, Georgia, furnished me with information on the Everitt family; Mrs. Marie Klein of Long Island, New York, did the same for the Mitchell family. Jerrell H. Shofner, Professor of History at the University of Central Florida, helped with the research and provided constant support as did Professor Bawa S. Singh of Florida State University. Professor Singh took the contemporary photographs of Pebble Hill that appear in this book. My wife, Miriam, and my friend, Hazel Richards, proved to be benign but observant auditors.

My work involved research at the National Archives at Washington, D. C., the Georgia Department of Archives and History, the University of Georgia, the University of North Carolina, the University of Florida, and Florida State University. At each of those institutions I was given friendly and professional help.

Finally, the history could not have been written without the encouragement and counsel of Mrs. Parker Poe, the last private owner of Pebble Hill. "Miss Pansy" was a wise, strong, and generous woman. She died on December 16, 1978.
William Warren Rogers
Tallahassee, Florida

JOHNSON–MITCHELL FAMILY

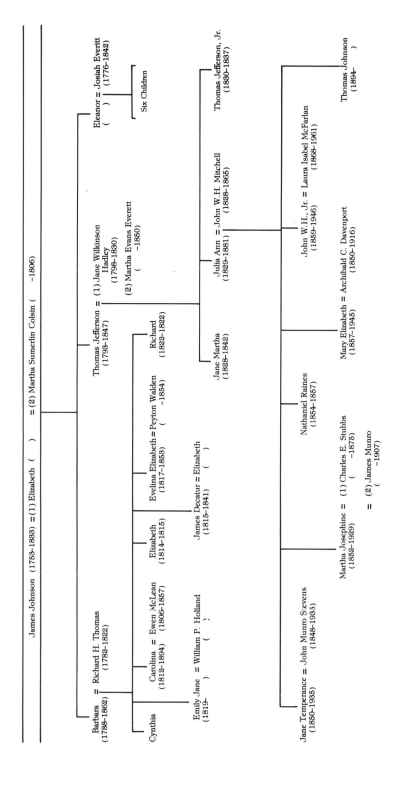

James Johnson (1758–1833) = (1) Elizabeth ( ) = (2) Martha Sumerlin Colsin (–1806)

Barbara (1788–1863) = Richard H. Thomas (1782–1822)

Cynthia

Carolina (1812–1894) = Ewen McLean (1806–1857)

Elizabeth (1814–1815)

Emily Jane = William P. Holland (1819–) (–)

James Decatur = Elizabeth (1815–1841) (–)

Evelina Elizabeth = Peyton Walden (1817–1853) (–1854)

Richard (1822–1822)

Thomas Jefferson (1798–1847) = (1) Jane Wilkinson Hadley (1798–1830)
= (2) Martha Evans Everett (–1850)

Eleanor = Josiah Everitt (–) (1776–1842)

Six Children

Jane Martha (1888–1842)

Julia Ann (1889–1881) = John W.H. Mitchell (1888–1865)

Thomas Jefferson, Jr. (1880–1887)

Jane Temperance = John Munro S-evens (1850–1935) (1848–1935)

Martha Josephine = (1) Charles E. Stubbs (1852–1929) (–1875)
= (2) James Munro (–1907)

Nathaniel Raines (1854–1857)

Mary Elizabeth = Archibald C. Davenport (1857–1945) (1850–1916)

John W. H., Jr. = Laura Isabel McFarlan (1859–1946) (1868–1961)

Thomas Johnson (1894–)

HANNA FAMILY

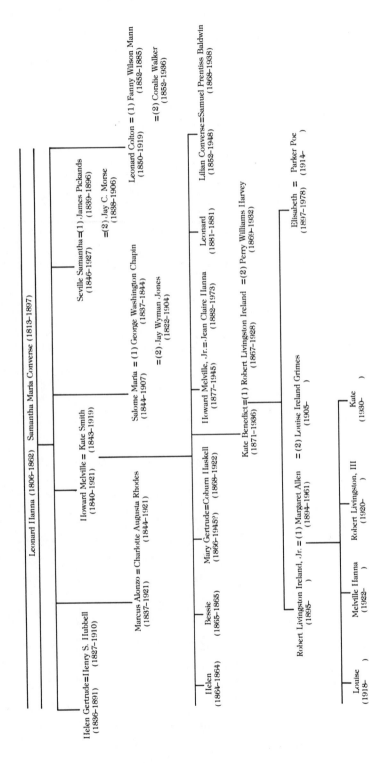

Historic Pebble Hill

Thomas County, Georgia

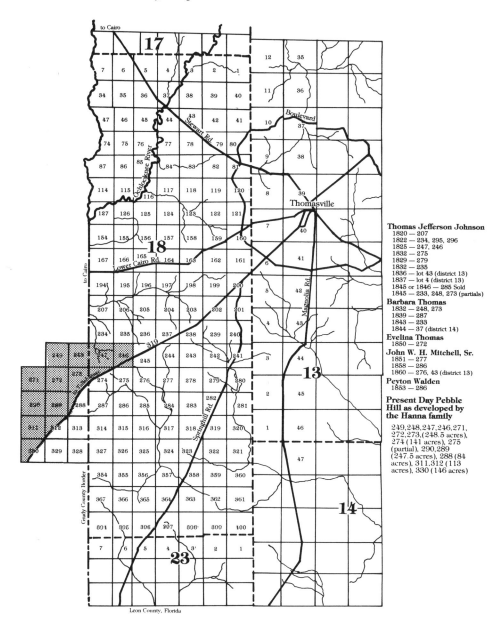

Thomas Jefferson Johnson
1820 — 207
1822 — 234, 295, 296
1825 — 247, 246
1832 — 275
1829 — 279
1832 — 235
1836 — lot 43 (district 13)
1837 — lot 4 (district 13)
1845 or 1846 — 285 Sold
1845 — 233, 248, 273 (partials)

Barbara Thomas
1832 — 248, 273
1839 — 287
1843 — 233
1844 — 37 (district 14)

Evelina Thomas
1850 — 272

John W. H. Mitchell, Sr.
1851 — 277
1858 — 286
1860 — 276, 43 (district 13)

Peyton Walden
1853 — 286

**Present Day Pebble
Hill as developed by
the Hanna family**

249, 248, 247, 246, 271,
272, 273, (248.5 acres),
274 (141 acres), 275
(partial), 290, 289
(247.5 acres), 288 (84
acres), 311, 312 (113
acres), 330 (146 acres)

Chapter I

THE SETTING

In early times Thomas County, which lies in extreme Southwest Georgia, was a favorite hunting site for the lower Creek and Apalachee Indians. Contemporary maps such as Delisle's *Carte Des Environs Du Mississippi* (1701) and his *Carte Du Mexique Et De La Floride* (1703) refer to the general region as "Apalache." The area, extending from the Chattahoochee River on the west to Wayne County on the east, took in the Okefenokee Swamp and skirted the big bend of the Ocmulgee and the Upper Altamaha rivers.[1] To the south lay the border of Florida and beyond that the peninsula's humid flat lands. What became Southwest Georgia was a slightly elevated general plain (although seldom rising over three hundred feet). Lower areas were strung with somber cypress swamps; numerous and unpredictable lime sinks formed chains of dark lakes outlined by birches, magnolias, and blackgums.

In Thomas County the topography became more varied, more undulated, resembling portions of north Georgia. The Aucilla, the Ochlocknee (the county's major river), and numerous streams and creeks wound their languid, narrow way— shallow except where occasional sandbars carved deeper pools— without apparent pattern. Frequently and unexpectedly, subterranean rivers burst forth as springs.

Forests of longleaf pine—straight and tall, pungent with the unmistakable scent of green needles and of resin—stretched endlessly across the land. Dogwoods, persimmons, sweetgums, magnolias, dwarf palmettoes, and wiregrass flourished in the moist but absorbent sandy soil. In certain small elevated places

---

[1]William Warren Rogers, *Ante-Bellum Thomas County 1825-1861* (Tallahassee, 1963), J. B. Clements, *History of Irwin County* (Atlanta, 1932), 17.

1

deposits of clay soil were concentrated, and from these hammocks sprang a profusion of hardwoods: water oaks, red and white and pin oaks, ashes, gums, maples, beeches, and hickories. If the towering longleaf pine (often rising over one hundred feet) had a rival for dominance, it was the equally impressive liveoak. Usually festooned with Spanish moss, the bearded liveoak grew with a dignified imperceptiveness—the dominant trunk often sent out branches larger than surrounding trees. Never completely shedding its elliptical leaves—dark green and leathery—an open standing liveoak seemed as much sculpted as alive and was at once brooding and inviting.[2]

Reigning as sovereigns over a domain abounding with fish and game were the red men. But without their knowledge, their proprietorship was doomed. The process began when the age of exploration and discovery, initiated in Europe in the fifteenth century, brought white men into the area. In 1539 the intrepid conquistador Hernando De Soto and his men landed at Tampa Bay, Florida. Moving north, the Spanish explorers crossed into Georgia in 1540. Their route carried them through or near Thomas County, and while De Soto did not linger, his sojourn enabled Spain to claim title to the region.[3]

Although Spain's imperial policy was motivated by a desire for economic gain, it had as well a broad religious base; the Catholic church, with its concomitant missionary and educational activities, tempered the quest for gold, land, and military victory. Spanish priests fanned out from San Augustin (St.

---

[2]S. W. McCallie, *Phosphates and Marls of Georgia* (Atlanta, 1896), 44-46. See also Hugh H. Bennett and Charles J. Mann, "Soil Survey of Thomas County, Georgia," *Field Operation of the Bureau of Soils* (n. p., n. d.).

[3]Herbert E. Bolton and Mary Ross, *The Debatable Land, A Sketch of the Anglo-Spanish Contest for the Georgia Country* (Berkeley, 1925), 6. See also Kathryn Abbey Hanna, *Florida Land of Change* (Chapel Hill, 1941), 14-15; and *Final Report of the United States De Soto Expedition Commission* (Washington, 1939), 344.

Augustine) and established a chain of missions throughout the Florida peninsula and parts of Georgia.[4]

The overwhelming presence of wildlife in the pervading forests had made the Apalache region a hunting preserve sparsely populated by humans. Because of this, the gentle and incongruous intrusion of missions did not directly affect the area. Yet at nearby San Luis (Tallahassee) the Spanish established an administrative and economic center. From this base they pushed westward to Pensacola and northward into Georgia. The Apalache country—with' its seemingly inexhaustible supply of deer, raccoons, fox, bears, squirrels, otters, and its infinite variety of birds, including wild turkeys—was the site of frequent hunting (and, increasingly, trading) expeditions by the Spanish.

Communication and transportation, other than by water, were difficult at best in the great Southern wilderness. Apparently the Spanish missions remained in contact by means of a vaguely defined path known as the Spanish Trail or "Camino Real." It followed a serpentine route from St. Augustine to present day Valdosta, Georgia, over to Thomas County and, bending south to Tallahassee, steered a westward course to Pensacola. By 1700 Spain had penetrated Southwest Georgia and for the time being had undisputed control.[5]

England got into the race for empire late, but early in the 1700's Carolina traders began encroaching on the Spanish fur monopoly. Although transients and trespassers, these wily backwoodsmen at least gave England a tenuous claim to parts of Georgia. Nor were the incursions always peaceful. In 1702 Carolina's governor, James Moore, laid siege to St. Augustine,

---

[4]Bolton and Ross, *Debatable Land*, 2-3. See also John Tate Lanning, *The Spanish Missions of Georgia* (Chapel Hill, 1935), *passim.*
[5]Folks Huxford. *The History of Brooks County, Georgia* (Athens, 1949), 1-2; Bolton and Ross, *Debatable Land*, 25-27.

and in 1704 he swept through Apalache destroying Spanish missions. England's shaky claims were strengthened in 1733 when James Oglethorpe and his band of settlers founded Savannah. Even though Oglethorpe had established the colony of Georgia, it did not include Southwest Georgia. The Englishman's grant, while it extended from "sea-to-sea," failed to encompass the territory south of the Altamaha River.[6]

England acquired full title to Georgia, curiously enough, as part of a military settlement with another major colonial power, France. The Caribbean region, Louisiana, the Mississippi Valley, and Canada had been the focus of France's New World penetration. Her position as a rival in the Western Hemisphere and in Europe to the thrust of England resulted in economic and military conflict. The disputes periodically fanned into fighting and culminated in the Seven Years' War, better known in America as the French and Indian War.

Spain was drawn into the conflict on the side of France, and following England's victory, was forced to pay the price of a defeated ally. The Treaty of Paris, drawn up in 1763, ended the war. Besides taking territorial concessions from France, England forced Spain to relinquish all land north of Florida. But even then Southwest Georgia did not come under the jurisdiction of the rest of the colony. The governor of South Carolina called attention to the original terms of the Carolina royal grant and assumed authority over the area. The settlers and traders acknowledged the control of South Carolina.[7]

Georgia and South Carolina quarreled over their exact boundary lines both in the north and the south. Not until well

---

[6]A trenchant and well written account is J. Lietch Wright, Jr., *Anglo-Spanish Rivalry in North America* (Athens, 1971), 60-73; see also Huxford, *Brooks County*, 2, and Verner W. Crane, *The Southern Frontier 1670-1732* (Durham, 1928), *passim.*

[7]James Etheridge Callaway, *The Early Settlement of Georgia* (Athens, 1948), 54.

after the American Revolution did the two states settle their differences. In 1787 the impasse ended when commissioners from both states met at Beaufort, South Carolina. After an agreement was made favoring South Carolina's claims in the north, the state gave up Southwest Georgia. At long last what became Thomas County was legally what it had been geographically all along: a part of Georgia.[8]

After the American Revolution, the United States worked to forge a viable government and assume a place of respect among the community of nations. Both England and France remained as potential threats, while in the South, Florida was still in the possession of Spain. Georgia played the uncomfortable and unwanted role of buffer between Florida and the United States, and the situation was exacerbated by the presence of the Indians.[9]

By 1800 the lower Creeks were the major tribe in the increasingly strategic area. Cajoled and encouraged by Spanish authorities, Indians moved across the ill-defined border from Florida. Attacking frontier settlements in Georgia, the Indians then retreated to the sanctuary of Spanish territory. Florida soon became a refuge not only for Indians but for runaway slaves, adventurers, outlaws, and the backwash of the rugged frontier. Angry Georgians demanded action to eliminate the threats against them. Even before the War of 1812 began Georgians led several abortive military expeditions into Florida. For obvious reasons these forays did not have the official sanction of the United States and achieved no permanent effects.[10]

---

[8]E. Merton Coulter, *A Short History of Georgia* (Chapel Hill, 1933), 178-179; David Duncan Wallace, *South Carolina A Short History* (Chapel Hill, 1951), 338.

[9]Coulter, *History of Georgia*, 196-197; see also Rembert W. Patrick, *Florida Fiasco* (Athens, 1954), *passim.*

[10]*Ibid.*

Most Georgians neither understood nor cared to understand the various issues—expansionist zeal, violation of neutral rights, economic ambitions, diplomatic blundering—that brought the United States and England into conflict once again. Yet the fact remained that the two nations became locked in combat in an uninspired and unpopular war. The lofty principles used to justify most wars seemed lacking in the struggle that was named for a year. For that matter, when the War of 1812 broke out, Georgia militiamen found themselves fighting the Indians rather than British regulars. Tecumseh, the able Shawnee chief, had come south as early as 1811, hoping to entice the Creeks and Seminoles into joining his Indian confederacy. The leader's persuasive talents brought the Upper Creeks of present day Alabama into an alliance with the British. But the Lower Creeks of Georgia spurned the appeals of Tecumseh. War on the frontier was bloody. In Alabama the Creeks or "Red Sticks" attacked Fort Mims in August 1813. Settlers from the surrounding countryside had taken refuge in the fort, and they, along with the soldiers garrisoned there, were massacred. The toll was 536 whites killed. Such savage encounters made other aspects of the War of 1812 seem almost gentlemanly.[11]

John Floyd and Georgia troops fought against the Creeks, but it was Andrew Jackson, the iron-hard and relentless Tennesseean, who decisively defeated the Indians. Although the Creeks fought valiantly, Jackson broke their power in March 1814, at the battle of Horseshoe Bend on the Tallapoosa River in Alabama. The territorial rewards of Old Hickory's victory were given diplomatic form by the Treaty of Fort Jackson, signed in August 1814. As outlined by the treaty, the Creeks

---

[11]Glenn Tucker, *Tecumseh Vision of Glory* (New York, 1956), 211, 281, 310; Peter J. Hamilton, *Colonial Mobile* (Boston and New York, 1898), 370.

gave up some twenty million acres of land: most of their domain in Alabama and southern Georgia along a strip of land approximately sixty miles wide. The Georgia land extended east from the Chattahoochee River at Fort Gaines, until it intersected the north-south line of lands previously ceded in 1802. This eastern terminus lay in what were then Wayne and Camden counties. The southern boundary was Florida.[12]

In truth, few people thought Georgia's new real estate had much potential. Strategically, the Treaty of Fort Jackson successfully cut off and isolated the Creeks from the Spaniards and Seminoles in Florida. Yet even that division would make for future trouble. Moreover, it was in Alabama not Georgia that the Creeks had given up most of their lands. Objective appraisals of the pine barrens and wiregrass of newly acquired Southwest Georgia were pessimistic: hostile Indians dwelled on the western side of the Chattahoochee River and to the south below the Florida boundary. Persistent rumors of bad water and malaria did little to enhance the picture. Not surprisingly, certain members of the state legislature, as an early Thomas County historian observed, were opposed to "spending the State's money trying to develop a country which God Almighty had left in an unfinished condition."[13]

It is probably fortunate that pioneers seldom listen to the objective appraisals of the less adventurous. They began moving into the new country. One writer who declared they "established their rude homes, and there lived for generations and generations, in unprogressive simplicity and strange isolation," indulged in an overstatement and drew an untenable generali-

---

[12]*American State Papers, Indian Affairs*, II (Washington, 1834), 493; Merritt B. Pound, *Benjamin Hawkins—Indian Agent* (Athens, 1951), 223-240; John K. Mahon, *The War of 1812* (Gainesville, 1972), 244.

[13]W. Irwin MacIntyre, *History of Thomas County Georgia* (Thomasville, 1923), 1.

zation.[14] Almost from the first, large plantations as well as small farms were developed.

After the War of 1812, Georgia caught the national mood: nationalism and expansion. Georgia was unique in that her debates and struggles over land titles were more significant and anguished than those of other Southern states. Despite having been an original colony, Georgia—especially Southwest Georgia—was caught up in the expansion of the 1820's that swept irresistably across Mississippi and Alabama. By the 1820's the profits from the cultivation of cotton were being realized; the potential of a textile industry was being propounded; a sturdy upland cotton plant, short stapled and capable of being grown all over the South, had been developed (in the coastal areas and parts of Thomas County Sea Island cotton could also be produced); and the pattern of a plantation economy based on the institution of Negro slavery had become entrenched. When all of these factors came together in the 1820's, they produced an insatiable demand for land.

Added to the dynamics of economics was the strong spirit of nationalism that emerged. Americans asserted themselves. The troublesome Florida issue was settled by the Adams-Onis Treaty of 1819, and the peninsula was added to the national domain; a protective tariff, favorable to American manufacturers, was passed; the Supreme Court under John Marshall rendered decisions establishing the dominance of national over state interests; a Second United States Bank was established; James Monroe, continuing the Virginia dynasty, was practically a concensus president; and while Americans spoke of an internal "Era of Good Feelings," possible external threats resulted in the enlargement of the military establishment. The American

---

[14]Harris Chappell, *Georgia History Stories* (New York, 1905), 346; see also Callaway, *Early Settlement of Georgia*, 108.

eagle was flexing its talons and just beginning to scream. Across the land ambitious citizens, confident of the future, were stirring, were on the move.[15]

Southwest Georgia was, at least in theory, free of Creek Indians' claims—in 1818 the Creeks made two additional grants of land: they sold one tract south of the Altamaha and Ocmulgee rivers and another at the headwaters of the Ocmulgee in north-central Georgia to the United States for $120,000.[16] Pioneer settlers, many with improper land titles and some with none, began moving in. The pattern of settlement was one of initial homesteading close to a river and then a gradual move into the quiet and lonely expanses of longleaf pine and wiregrass. The first roads followed old Indian trails. Some three or four of these routes converged on what would become Thomas County, and from there extended southward into Florida. But the settlers also hacked rude roads as they went, facing the danger of attack from Indians who resented the invasion of their hunting lands and who disagreed with the treaties forced upon their tribal leaders.

The Georgia and Florida boundary was still not clear (the question of the exact line remained in controversy throughout the ante-bellum period). Early settlers of Southwest Georgia—hailing from Pulaski, Burke, Bulloch, Screven, Laurens, Montgomery, and other older counties—set for themselves the myriad tasks of turning an unspoiled hunting preserve into a region of farms and villages. On the rich hammock lands near the Florida demarcation, the settlers who had been cattle and wood rangers soon became farmers. As more settlers

---

[15]See George Dangerfield, *The Era of Good Feelings* (New York, 1952), *passim.*

[16]Huxford, *Brooks County*, 3; Robert S. Cotterill, *The Southern Indians. The Story of the Civilized Tribes Before Removal* (Norman, 1954), 209-210.

came in and the population grew, the inevitable demands were heard for the establishment of counties.[17]

Responding to the pressure, the state legislature passed an act on December 15, 1818, creating three sprawling counties: Early, Irwin, and Appling. Provision was made for the counties to be surveyed into land lots and districts. As designated, lots in Early County contained 250 acres each, and the districts were twelve miles and forty chains square. Even larger provisions were established for Irwin and Appling, where the lots consisted of 490 acres each and the districts were twenty miles and ten chains square. In each of the three counties a fractional lot was one containing less than 160 acres.[18] The next year the legislature provided for the organization of the counties: election sites were designated and certain citizens were empowered to superintend the election of justices to the Inferior Courts which, in turn, were to transact business and select locations for county sites. Carrying out the act's provisions took time, but by 1820 the elections had been held, the courts formed, and the counties existed in fact as well as name.[19]

Crucial to the area's development was the disposition of the land. In 1777 Georgia passed a land act establishing a "headright" system (the head of a family received two hundred acres of land; after the survey but before the grant he was to clear and cultivate three out of each hundred acres; he could also purchase additional land). Another land act in 1783 continued the headright system. The state's new constitution of 1789 provided that justices of the peace could issue land

---

[17]Huxford, *Brooks County*, 4; George Gillman Smith, *The Story of Georgia and the Georgia People 1733 to 1860* (Macon, 1900), 405-406.

[18]Lucium Q. C. Lamar, *A Compilation of the Laws of the State of Georgia. . . Since the Year 1810 to the Year 1819. . .* (Augusta, 1921), 416, 425.

[19]*Ibid.*, 236-238; Clements, *Irwin County*, 30-31; Huxford, *Brooks County*, 8.

warrants; the justices of a county constituted a land court that met regularly to confirm land grants. The grants were then signed by the governor. Although subject to several amendments, Georgia's headright law remained in effect until 1909.

The area encompassed by Early, Irwin, and Appling counties was distributed initially in conformity with another system of appropriating the public domain: the land lottery. Of Georgia's six land lotteries, it was the third, also known as the 1820 lottery, that affected the three new counties. The system was relatively simple: after the surveys were completed and the land divided into districts and lots, the surveyor-general had prepared small cards, each containing the number of one of the land lots. Inferior Court justices from each of the state's thirty-nine counties submitted to the governor the names of all persons eligible to draw in the lottery. Eligibility was based on twelve classifications. The largest included married men who had resided in the state for three years. Men in this category were entitled to two draws. Similarly qualified bachelors were permitted one draw each, and also included were veterans of the Revolutionary War, War of 1812, and Indian wars. Widows and families of orphans were allowed to participate, but persons who had obtained land from previous lotteries were excluded (except for invalid or indigent Revolutionary War veterans).[20]

The lottery drawings lasted for several weeks and were held at the state capitol at Milledgeville. The name cards for Early County's twenty-six districts, Irwin's sixteen, and Appling's thirteen, were placed in one large revolving drum.

---

[20]Alexander M. Hitz of Atlanta has made a careful compilation of those people who received land in the 1820 lottery that eventually became Thomas County. His list also includes information concerning the 1827 and 1832 land lotteries.

Cards bearing the lot numbers were placed in another, and after the drums were spun vigorously, cards were drawn from both. The person whose name was extracted became entitled to the land lot whose number had been drawn. All he had to do was pay a grant fee of $18 and the land was his. Since there were always far more names than lots, the person whose name came up before the supply of lots was exhausted was known as a "fortunate drawer." If the grant fee remained unpaid, the land reverted to the state as of September 1841. Education for poor children was at least theoretically assured by the reservation of land lots number 10 and 100 for their benefit. There was no drawing on fractional lots which were sold at public auctions by commissioners appointed by the governor.[21]

Most settlers preferred the headright system to that of the lottery, but the settling of Southwest Georgia would have proceeded regardless of what system was used. Many pioneers pushed ahead of surveyors and selected homesites and constructed log cabins. In truth, a majority of the so-called fortunate drawers had no intention of actually settling in the area: they kept their grants for speculative purposes. The actual settlers had to assume the inconvenient and confusing task of locating the legal owners and purchasing the land from them.[22]

The newly designated counties—Early on the west, Irwin in the middle, and Appling on the east—were not intended to have permanent geographical lines. It was understood that as people moved in, smaller units would be created. To this end in 1823 Representative Richard Spann of Early County introduced a bill creating Decatur County. The new unit was to be carved out of the southern part of his own constituency

---

[21]*Ibid.*
[22]Huxford, *Brooks County*, 8.

and to consist of land districts 14 through 20, and 22, 23, and 27. Named for naval hero Stephen Decatur, the new county received the necessary endorsement from fiery Governor George M. Troup. In the next few years the county seat of Bainbridge was established and settlement continued.[23]

An early settler, one Martin Hardin (sometimes spelled Harden) was elected in 1824 as the first representative to the state legislature from Decatur County. Hardin was a leading citizen, and, along with Duncan Ray and others, had been named in the act creating Decatur County to select a site for the county seat. In the meantime more settlers pushed in. In his bid for reelection in 1825, Hardin was confronted with the issue of creating still another county. Because he lived in western Decatur, Hardin did not champion the establishment of a new division to the east. The incumbent's opponent, a man with the distinctive name of Thomas Jefferson Johnson, owned property in the east and based his candidacy on the need for a new political unit. The issue became central to the campaign, and Johnson was elected.[24]

It was this man, Thomas Jefferson Johnson, who would become the father of Thomas County and the master of Pebble Hill plantation.

---

[23]*Acts of Georgia 1823*, 57-60; MacIntyre, Thomas County, 24; Frank S. Jones, *History Of Decatur County Georgia* (Atlanta, 1971), 182.

[24]Jones, *Decatur County*, 260, 265; Thomasville *Press*, April 14, 1930, reprinted an important sketch of Thomas County; written around 1880 by Janes L. Seward, a county leader, who died in 1886, the sketch is invaluable for early recollections.

Chapter II

COUNTY AND TOWN

Ambitious, strong-willed, definite in purpose, a seeker of perfection, able to inspire confidence in others—such are the characteristics attributed to those born under the sign of Capricorn. Students of astrology might make a case for the signs of the Zodiac in the person of Thomas Jefferson Johnson. Born January 17, 1793, he was the son of James Johnson (a durable individual who lived to be eighty-one) and Martha Summerlin Colson who died in 1806. James Johnson's first wife, Elizabeth, died at the birth of her first child. She and the baby were buried in Virginia. James and Martha's oldest child was a girl, Barbara, born May 18, 1788. In many ways Barbara, who also came to Thomas County, was as remarkable as Thomas Jefferson Johnson. A third child, Eleanor, about whom little is known, also migrated to Southwest Georgia with her husband.

The Johnsons originally came to America from Annandale, Scotland, and settled in Sussex and Prince George counties, Virginia. James Johnson fought in the Revolutionary War, serving as captain of a Virginia company from Lunenburg County. Some time later, probably in the 1790's Johnson moved from Virginia to Georgia and established his family in Pulaski County, a region that was part of the territory ceded by the Creek Indians and created in 1808.[1]

The village of Hawkinsville, some forty miles south of Macon, was the county seat. James Johnson was more closely connected with Hartford, a settlement east of Hawkinsville

---

[1] See Mrs. Wallace Leigh Harris (Virginia Speer) (Compiler), *History of Pulaski and Bleckley Counties, Georgia 1808-1856* (Macon, 1957 (2 vols., second volume published in 1958)), II, 69-71; and Hawkinsville Chapter Daughters Of The American Revolution (Compiler), *History of Pulaski County Georgia* (Atlanta, 1935), 11-27; notes in Hopkins Collection.

across the Ocmulgee River. Johnson prospered as a planter, and passed his farming abilities along to his son. Young Thomas Jefferson Johnson grew into manhood in Pulaski County where he found life pleasant and, periodically, exciting. The pleasure came from hunting and fishing and being part of a well-to-do family. Excitement was furnished by militia service. Elaborately organized from the state down to the local level, the militia attracted most able bodied males and offered protection against possible Indian attack and such other domestic disturbances as might occur. Reputations could be made that had social and political benefits, and at the very least musters of local companies were colorful and important social events eagerly anticipated.

The young Thomas Johnson served his time as a citizen soldier. In July 1812, a cavalry company of twenty-eight men was organized in Pulaski County. The unit was commanded by Captain Richard H. Thomas, husband of Johnson's sister, Barbara. Johnson served as first sergeant. Part of the service entailed construction of a road. Less essential but much more interesting was the time spent in reconnoitering on the frontier of Wayne and Camden counties.[2] Twice in 1813 Johnson was called to militia duty. His service of twelve days, from March 29, to April 9, earned him $6.20 (Richard Thomas got $23 as company commander).[3] Johnson served most of November that fall working as a private in Major Elijah Blackshear's expedition. The men labored laying off and marking out a proposed road from Hartford to Camp Pinckney on the St. Mary's River. Also serving as a private was Richard Mitchell, a young friend of Johnson's who would later join him in the move to Thomas County.[4]

---

[2]Mrs. J. E. Hayes (Arranger), *Georgia Military Affairs*, III (1801-1813), 119-121; see the same Arranger's *Georgia Military Record Book 1779-1839*, 289-290.

[3]Hayes, *Georgia Military Affairs*, III (1801-1813), 164-165.

[4]Hayes, *Georgia Military Record Book 1779-1839*, 281.

From November 9, to November 22, 1814, Johnson performed his last militia service for Pulaski County. He was part of a detachment of Georgia cavalry and mounted riflemen under Lieutenant Colonel Allen Took with Captain Richard H. Thomas second in command. Once again, Johnson's rank was that of first sergeant.[5]

After the War of 1812 ended Johnson became less absorbed with martial glory and more concerned with the challenge offered by the newly opened lands of Southwest Georgia. There Johnson would have the opportunity to build and develop a plantation as his father had done in Pulaski County. Before tracing Johnson's family life, how he established Pebble Hill plantation, and the important role he played in the region's development, his authorship of the bill creating Thomas County and his part in founding Thomasville need to be set in order.

After defeating Martin Hardin for the right to represent Decatur County in the state legislature, Johnson was true to his word. He had scarcely taken his seat before he presented the solons at Milledgeville with a bill creating Thomas County. Johnson's proposal followed a familiar routine: it was read twice in the House, sent to the Senate for similar treatment, and then passed by the legislature on November 30. The creation of a county to the east, Lowndes, was coupled in the same bill. The measure became law—complete with the graceful signatures of Thomas V. Murray, Speaker of the House, Allen B. Powell, President of the Senate, and Governor George M. Troup—on December 3, 1825. The new entity was taken from the Seventeenth and Eighteenth districts of Decatur County and from those parts of the Twenty-third and Nineteenth Districts lying

---

[5]Hayes, *Georgia Military Affairs*, IV (1814-1819), 196. See *ibid.*, 185, which lists one Thomas Johnson (no middle initial) as a private in November 1814, in a militia detachment from Pulaski County. See also Hayes, *Georgia Military Record Book 1779-1839*, 125-128, 148.

Thomas Jefferson Johnson
(1793-1847)
and his wife,
Jane Wilkinson Hadley
(1798-1829)

on the east side of the Ochlocknee River. The rest of Thomas was formed from the Thirteenth and Fourteenth districts of Irwin County.[6]

Various boundary changes would come later. On December 27, 1826, the Eighth District of Lowndes was added to Thomas. A major adjustment in the county's geography occurred in 1858 with the creation of Brooks County, formed from Thomas and Lowndes. Then in 1905, Grady County was created from Thomas and Decatur.[7]

The fledgling counties of Thomas and Lowndes were organized on December 24, 1825, when the legislature directed two or more justices of the peace (who were not candidates) to hold elections for justices of the Inferior Courts. The elected justices were to provide for the election of other county officials. Five commissioners were named to select a county seat for Thomas, purchase land for the site, and lay off lots for sale to the public. The early commissioners were Duncan Ray, William J. Forson, Simon Hadley, Sr., Michael Horn and John ("Thomas" was possibly his true name) Hill Bryan. The place for holding the Superior and the Inferior courts and the elections was to be the home of Charles Kingsley.[8]

---

[6]Lowndes was formed from the Eighth, Ninth, Tenth, Eleventh, Twelfth, Fifteenth and Sixteenth districts of Irwin. See *Journal of the Georgia House of Representatives. . . 1825*, 37, 40, 47, 55, 64, 88, 92; *Acts of Georgia 1825* 54. Savannah *Georgian*, December 30; 1825; Macon *Messenger*, November 9, 16, 23, December 7, 14, 1825; General James Jackson Chapter, D.A.R., *History of Lowndes County, Georgia, 1825-1941* (Valdosta, 1941), 1; Jane Twitty Shelton, *Pines And Pioneers A History Of Lowndes County, Georgia 1825-1900* (Atlanta, 1976), 53.

[7]Other smaller changes occurred in 1850 when a land lot in Baker County was added to Thomas. Thomas obtained another land lot in 1859 from Mitchell County which had been formed from Baker. Thomas and Lowndes counties also gave up land in 1856 for the creation of Colquitt County, and in 1859 and 1870 Thomas yielded small amounts of land to Colquitt as well. For convenience see Mary Givens Bryan (Compiler), *Georgia Official and Statistical Register 1957-1958* (Hapeville, 1958), 671-678.

[8]*Acts of Georgia 1825*, 55.

Soon the commissioners, with the exception of Thomas Hill Bryan who had died, began their search. Besides securing a central location, the men took into consideration both topography and the availability of water. In June 1826, they selected a site for the county seat: Lot 39 which lay in the Thirteenth District of Irwin County and contained 490 acres. The man from whom the lot was purchased was Thomas Jefferson Johnson. He had owned the lot only a month, and at first glance it would appear that Johnson had created a fief for himself and was boldly engaging in the time honored practice of land speculation.

But such was not the case. In the land lottery of 1820 one Ziber Fletcher of Monroe County had been the original drawee of Lot 39. In May 1826, Johnson paid Fletcher $200 for the acreage. Apparently he considered the land suitable as the seat of government for the new county. Whatever the case, the commissioners agreed. They offered Johnson $210 and he accepted. Johnson, with full knowledge of the potential value of property in the future Thomasville, sold his land for a modest profit of $10.[9]

It might be assumed that Johnson, even if he refused to take advantage of his favored position in selling Lot 39, would, once the town was surveyed, buy and sell various plots of land. Yet his participation was extremely limited. He bought a lot in the village from the commissioners in the fall of 1826. His purchase price of $50 was intended as much as anything to encourage other buyers. Six years later he sold the lot for $100.[10] In 1835 Johnson sold a half-acre lot in Thomasville to

---

[9]Deed Record Book A, Thomas County, Circuit Clerk's Office, Thomas County Courthouse, Thomasville, 73-75; 140-142; Deed Record Book A-1, *ibid.*, 29-30; in a separate indenture Blancy Fletcher, wife of Ziber, relinquished any claims to Lot 39. See Deed Record Book A, 75, and Deed Record Book A-1, 29-30, *ibid.*

[10]Deed Record Book B, *ibid.*, 120-121.

John Parramore for $125.[11] Other than these two transactions, Johnson refrained from buying and selling land in Thomasville. He seemed more interested in having settlers move in than he was in making money out of land sales.

With the land purchased for a town, the commissioners informed Milledgeville of their action, and on December 22, 1826, the state legislature made it official. That body declared "the courthouse and jail of said County of Thomas is hereby made permanent at a place now known and called by the name of Thomasville, and shall be called and known by that name."[12]

A question would be raised in later years concerning the origins of the names Thomas and Thomasville.[13] It seems almost certain that Johnson was responsible for both designations. As previously discussed, Johnson's brother-in-law and commanding officer in the Pulaski County militia was Richard H. Thomas. Barbara Johnson and Thomas were married on January 23, 1812. Although he had risen to the rank of colonel by 1819 (on accepting his appointment from Governor William Rabun, he pledged himself to uphold the constitution of Georgia and, in a separate statement, swore that he had not engaged in a duel since the previous July), Thomas had an even more renowned relative: General Jett Thomas. It is not certain that

[11]Deed Record Book E. *ibid.*, 22.

[12]*Acts of Georgia 1826*, 173.

[13]The descendants of Lewis Ashton Thomas, in a claim of May 10, 1954, asserted that the county was named for their ancestor. They filed documentary evidence that Lewis A. Thomas was a member of the Grand Jury, Decatur District, in 1826, and owned a large plantation just west of present Thomasville. The claim was based further on the testimony of various descendants. Thomas was born in North Carolina about 1772. In 1814 he moved to Laurens County, Georgia. From there he came to Southwest Georgia. The claim was filed by William Knox Fitzpatrick and is in the Department of Archives and History, Atlanta. Additional letters supporting the claims are in the Elizabeth F. Hopkins Collection, Thomas County Historical Society, Thomasville.

Johnson knew Jett Thomas personally, but it is highly probable that he did. Born in Virginia, Jett had migrated to Georgia with his father soon after the American Revolution. A noted architect who designed and built the old State House at Milledgeville and the first building of the state university at Athens, Jett Thomas also served as an artillery commander in the War of 1812. He saw action under General Floyd against the Indians. Unfortunately, Thomas developed an eye ailment that was cancerous and caused his death in 1817.[14]

In the meantime, Barbara and Richard Thomas remained in Pulaski County and began their family. Richard died July 17, 1822, and later, in December 1827, Barbara and her children moved to Thomas County to be near her father and brother. Because of family connections and the contributions to Georgia by General Jett Thomas, Thomas Jefferson Johnson suggested that both the county and town might appropriately be named for him, and this was done.[15]

There was also the question, much more difficult to resolve, of who was the first white settler in Thomas County. It is not possible to ascertain who brought the first slave into the region. People began moving into the area before 1820. Among the first was Thomas Hill Bryan who migrated by way of North Carolina and Middle Georgia about 1819. His entry was accomplished before there was a road. A man of pride and ability, Bryan had the first hewn log house in the area, and while cabins built later often had clay floors, his were covered with hewn puncheons. If not Thomas County's initial settler, Bryan was already there when most of the others arrived. Around

---

[14]See statement of Judge John W. H. Mitchell, grandson of Thomas Jefferson Johnson, in "Golden Jubilee" issue of Thomasville *Times Enterprise*, November 11, 1929. See also George White, *Statistics of the State of Georgia* (Savannah, 1849), 545-547.

[15]*Ibid.*

1840 his son, Hardy Bryan, built a two-story residence in Thomasville that was probably the town's first such structure.[16]

The county's growth continued. Aaron Everitt (the Everitt or Everett family was large, industrious, and able) was employed to lay off and survey a courthouse square and adjacent lots in Thomasville. Soon the lots were offered at public sale, although they brought less than land boom prices.[17] The town became an outpost in a pine wilderness by the late 1820s. A courthouse was built of roughly split pine logs, and in November 1827, was the scene of the first session of the Superior Court. Among other business before the courts was the sentencing of three Indians to be hanged for the crime of murder. The small village had a few dwellings. E. J. Perkins had a home and a grocery. Nearby was another home, and James Kirksey operated a store, which, unfortunately, fell victim to the first fire in Thomasville's history. One of the earliest stores was operated by Simon A. Smith and his son.[18]

Another of Thomas Hill Bryan's sons, Loverd (Lovard), and his intended, Elizabeth Wyche, daughter of Littleton and Susannah Wyche, were probably the first white couple to get married in Thomas County. On June 30, 1826, the day of the marriage, Thomas County existed officially, but there was no courthouse and there were no officers. The determined Bryan gave bond for the subsequent procurement of a license and persuaded an official of Decatur County to perform the ceremony.[19]

---

[16]Bryan's will, probated in 1826, revealed that he owned land in both Irwin and Early counties. See Thomasville *Times*, December 11, 1875, quoting Macon *Telegraph*. The Hopkins Collection contains information taken from Bryan's will revealing his ownership of Lot 13, Thirteenth District of Irwin, and Lot 339, Seventeenth District of Early.

[17]MacIntyre, *Thomas County*, 2-3; "Seward's Sketch."

[18]MacIntyre, *Thomas County*, 5-6; Augusta *Centennial* Chronicle, May 9, 1885; "Seward's Sketch." United Daughters of the Confederacy Historical Collection, IV (Thomasville, 1932), n. p., has his letter of appointment.

[19]Unidentified newspaper clipping dated July 19, 1879, in Hopkins Collection.

Carolina Slade was the first white child born in the county. Her parents, the Rev. and Mrs. John Slade, lived in the rear of Perkins's one-room log house. Born in 1827 or 1828, Carolina was named in honor of South Carolina's resistance to the tariff and was often called the "little nullifier."[20]

A child's birth was an indication of permanence; in less human terms so was the incorporation of the town in 1831. Appointed as Thomasville's first commissioners were Isaac P. Brooks, Edward Remington, Malcolm Ferguson, James Kirksey, and Murdock McAwley.[21] Men like Johnson who wished to come to town had to take roughly outlined bridle paths, but improvements were on the way.

As the county developed, sporadic difficulties with the Indians continued. Despite the Treaty of Fort Jackson and the limited number of Indians living in Thomas County, the citizens shared with their Southwest Georgia neighbors the danger of physical attack. The chief means of defense were familiar: local volunteer militia companies, who often summoned similar units from nearby counties, and federal troops.

That the Indians who passed through the county received exemplary treatment from the white settlers is open to doubt. Yet during the county's first year of existence there were Indian raids on isolated homes, repeated thefts of livestock, and actual murders. Early in December 1826, a white settler's family was slain at their cabin just across the Florida line. Thomas Jefferson Johnson wrote Governor Troup that "I collected a few men who had no families to take care of and set out for the scene of the murder. . . ." Some militia units

---

[20]See "An Old Citizen" to Thomasville *Times,* January 22, 1881. For other remarks about early settlers and births see *ibid.,* January 15, 1881.

[21]*Acts of Georgia 1831,* 237-238; MacIntyre, *Thomas County,* 3.

24

arrived before Johnson, and so the owner of Pebble Hill turned back.[22]

Johnson explained that it was difficult to maintain a standing militia company in the county because arms were scarce and, more importantly, because most men were unwilling to be away from their families. Johnson believed that many men would agree to scout for a few days. For them to do even that it would be good, Johnson suggested, to construct two forts as places "of refuge in case of danger for the women and children." Noting the Creeks to the north and the Seminoles to the south, "we may be said to have a frontier on two sides," he lamented. Johnson concluded that because of "the sparseness of our population together with the general treatment and bad conduct of both tribes of Indians on our frontier— I believe we stand very much in need of some efficient assistance which I do hope will be afforded us."[23]

Governor Troup responded positively to Johnson's request. He sent in a state expedition that remained from December 19, 1826, to January 25, 1827. Captain R. N. Hicklin and his cavalry company of sixty-seven men called their Thomas County post Camp Defiance.[24] Trouble subsided, and the troops were withdrawn.

Again in 1831, the state militia was dispatched to Thomas County. Without facilities to remain permanently; the soldiers departed shortly, but they left their arms and ammunition in the custody of Thomas J. Johnson. A special act of the legislature instructed Johnson to turn over the arms to any volunteer company formed in the county.[25]

---

[22]*Creek Indian Letters Talks And Treaties*, III, types and bound volumes in the Georgia Department of Archives and History has Johnson's letter to Troup dated December 8, 1826.

[23]*Ibid.*

[24]Hayes, *Georgia Military Affairs*, V (1820-1829), 239-241.

[25]*Acts of Georgia 1831*, 306-307.

Occasional skirmishes gave way to general conflict in the mid-1830's. Known as the Second Seminole War, its encounters were not limited to Florida. Driven together by adversity, Creeks and Seminoles made common cause. From time to time small groups of Creeks left Alabama and, using Southwest Georgia as a gateway, joined forces with the Seminoles in Florida. To meet the mounting difficulties, Thomas countians gathered in January 1836 and formed a cavalry company known as the Georgia Guards. It was commanded by Captain Joseph S. Neely. The wisdom of such action was soon demonstrated. In May the Creeks committed atrocities in Georgia's Stewart County, and the Seminoles made hostile demonstrations at Monticello, across the Florida line in Jefferson County. Neely's mounted company was quickly sent from Thomasville to Monticello as a precautionary move in case fighting broke out.[26]

A body of Creeks was reported in Southwest Georgia in June 1836, and still another cavalry company was formed in Thomas County. Captain James A. Newman commanded the forty-six man unit that got a quick test of fire. Newman's company joined other Georgia and Florida militiamen in a battle against the Creeks in Baker County, Georgia. Occurring in early July, the encounter was a victory for the militia: 13 Indians were killed, about 150 captured, and the remainder fled into the countryside.[27]

Only a few days later the fighting was renewed at the Battle of Brushy Creek in Lowndes (present-day Cook) County. Captain Newman's company joined one from Lowndes County under the combined command of Thomas County's Michael Young. Also engaged in the fighting were two other companies:

[26]Savannah *Georgian*, May 31, 1836; Hayes, *Georgia Military Affairs*, VII (1836), 97-98; Huxford, *Brooks County*, 35-37; Thomas County File, Georgia Department of Archives and History.
[27]Tallahassee *Floridian*, June 18, 1836; Colonel Thomas E. Blackshear to Governor William Schley, July 8, 1836, Thomas County File, GDAH.

one from Lowndes and one from Thomas under Captain H. C. Tucker. As Thomas County's Thomas E. Blackshear, Colonel of the Sixty-Ninth Regiment, reported later to Governor William Schley, the Indians were defeated. Twenty-two Indians and two of their Negro allies were killed; many Indians were wounded, while eighteen women and children were taken as prisoners to the Thomas County jail. Two militiamen, including Barton Ferrell of Thomas, were killed and nine were wounded. A few days later the Indians who had escaped were trapped in a surprise attack and either killed or captured.[28] The Savannah *Georgian* commented that the Brushy Creek affair reflected "the highest credit upon the gallantry and good conduct of our citizen soldiers of Thomas and Lowndes."[29]

Caught in a geographical crossfire, sixteen prominent citizens petitioned the governor on August 3. They asked for protection because the "County of Thomas is at this time the frontier both on the North & the South."[30] But the worst was over. Thomas County militia units saw limited action in the next few years, and federal troops stationed in Southwest Georgia helped deter future attacks. For that matter, regular soldiers and the militia did not get along. In any case, Thomas countians proved effective as citizen soldiers, and there was little difficulty after the late 1830's.[31] The involvement of Johnson and his fellow citizens was as participants at the conclusion of an inevitable, but brutal, process; one that ended with land being forcibly taken from the Indians with compen-

---

[28]Savannah *Georgian*, July 30, 1836; Tallahassee *Floridian*, July 30, 1836; for slightly differing versions see White, *Statistics of Georgia*, 648-650; and James Jackson Chapter, *Lowndes County*, 11-13; Shelton, *History of Lowndes County*, 66-67.

[29]Savannah *Georgian*, July 30, 1836.

[30]Mss. petition to William Schley, August 3, 1836, Thomas County file, GDAH.

[31]Rogers, *Ante-Bellum Thomas County*, 38-39.

sation that was either absent or inadequate. The most graphic form it took was resettlement of the Indians in the West.

All the while, progress in Thomas County was, if not spectacular, steady. A visitor in the 1830's wrote, "Thomasville was ... some improvement on Bainbridge, but its architecture was on the same order, purely log style, with but very few specimens of domestic, ecclesiastical or educational buildings. Glass windows were a luxury that did not appear to be generally prevalent, if indeed, there were any there at all. The town consisted of a small collection of log structures set down in the midst of a vast pine forest, which gave one the feeling of isolation from the outside world, which seemed to lay at an infinite distance beyond its boundless screen of primeval woods."[32]

---

[32]See "C. B." to "My Dears, Charlies, Jim, and the Great-Grand Baby," quoted in Thomasville *Times Enterprise* September 7, 1895. The letter was written from San Francisco, California. Marion R. Hemperley, Georgia Surveyor General Department, Atlanta, Georgia, has written a brief but informative history of the old roads of Thomas County. See copy in the files of Thomasville Landmarks, Thomasville.

Chapter III

THOMAS JEFFERSON JOHNSON AND PEBBLE HILL

Johnson had already acquired the 250 acres that comprised land Lot 246 (originally Early, then Decatur, then Thomas), the property on which he would build Pebble Hill—as well as other land—when he got married on March 8, 1827. In his mid-thirties, firmly established as a respected planter, Johnson vividly impressed Jane Wilkinson Hadley.

Johnson's bride came from a pioneer Southern family. Jane was named for her mother (born June 29, 1767, place unknown, died November 27, 1829). She also had two brothers—Samuel, born 1796, died 1850, and Simon, Jr., whose dates of birth and death are unknown—and a sister, Anne, born 1809, died 1824. The most remarkable member of the family was her father, Simon Hadley, Sr. Born in North Carolina in 1760, Hadley was in his teens when he joined the militia to fight the British. By the time the Revolutionary War ended, he had served four enlistments and seen action as a scout, spy, and procurer of beef cattle for the colonials. In the early years of the Republic, Hadley moved to Burke County, Georgia. He next lived in Montgomery County which he represented in the state House of Representatives in 1824 and the extra session of 1825. He finally settled in Thomas County and became prominent. In 1830 Hadley's 48 bondsmen ranked him as the second largest slaveowner in the county. He was one of the 5 commissioners who selected a site for the county seat, and, along with Johnson, was a member of the county's first grand jury. Hadley was elected as Thomas County's first representative to the state legislature.[1]

---

[1]See Hadley family biographical folder in Thomas County Historical Society Collection; additional information is located in the Hopkins Collection.

29

Family cemetery at the rear of the home

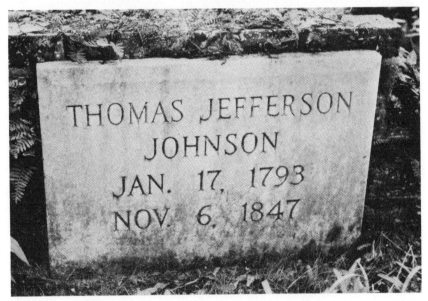

Headstone of Thomas Jefferson Johnson

Jane was born November 15, 1798, and she, like other members of the Hadley family, well knew the hardships and pleasures of frontier life. Her admiration for Johnson soon turned to love, and at the age of twenty-nine she accepted the responsibilities of looking after the household activities of an expanding plantation and rearing a family.

The marriage of Johnson and Jane Hadley was marked by its brevity and tragedy. Their first child, Jane Martha, was born March 27, 1828. Julia Ann was born a little more than a year later, June 7, 1829. In the fall of that year Jane's mother, Jane Wilkinson Hadley, died. As a father, Johnson took understandable pride in his daughters, but he also wanted a son. To his great pleasure Jane gave birth to a boy on September 12, 1830. The father had scarcely got around to telling his friends about young Thomas Jefferson Johnson, Jr., when his happiness turned to shock and heartbreak. The birth of the baby must have been accompanied by severe complications because less than two weeks later, on September 22, the mother died. Jane was only thirty-two years old. Johnson buried her, as was the custom, in what would become a family burying grounds located to the rear of Pebble Hill.

Johnson was left a widower with three small children to care for. During the next years he threw himself single-mindedly into his work. Even so, there was no escaping intermittent periods of sadness. On December 3, 1833, his father, indomitable despite the loss of his eyesight, died and was buried in the family cemetery. Then on May 14, 1836, Simon Hadley, Sr., died. Johnson's father-in-law was buried in a rural county cemetery beside his wife and daughter. Not without cause was Hadley's tombstone inscribed with the words "A Great 75 Years." In 1837 young Thomas Jefferson, Jr., visited friends at LaGrange in Troup County. While there he was stricken with the dreaded typhoid fever. The seven-year-old never returned home. He died on the afternoon of June 10, and was buried at LaGrange.[2]

Somehow Johnson was able to withstand his personal losses. His difficulties were made easier when on December 14, 1839, he married for the second time. His new wife, Martha Evans Everett, was a widow. Not much is known about Martha. Although the chances of error exist, Thomas County marriage records list the spelling of her name as Everett rather than Everitt. Even so, it is possible that she was the widow of Aaron Everitt who died in 1837. Aaron was the brother of Josiah Everitt who lived in Decatur County and was the brother-in-law of Thomas Jefferson Johnson.[3] No children would be born to Johnson and Martha Evans, but their marriage was a good one. It was soon marred by another death. In the summer of 1842, on August 17, tragedy struck Jane Martha, Johnson's first born. Only fourteen, Jane Martha died at three in the morning. While the causes were not given, death was probably due to a sudden illness.[4]

As befitted a man of his judgment, Johnson recognized his own mortality, and in 1843 drew his will. Leaving the bulk of his estate to Martha Evans, he required one condition of his wife: his daughter Julia Ann was to live with her until

---

[2]Some accounts state that young Johnson was already sick and was sent to LaGrange to recuperate.

[3]The author is indebted to Mrs. May A. Walton of Augusta, Georgia for the use of her biographical information on the Everitt family.

[4]The genealogical information is based primarily on the family Bible of Thomas Jefferson Johnson and Jane W. Hadley. The Bible's family records were transcribed August 6, 1937, by Elizabeth F. Hopkins and were in the possession of John W. H. Mitchell, Jr., of Thomasville. Grandson of Thomas Jefferson Johnson, Mitchell was the author of a useful "Sketch of Pebble Hill." Information was also obtained from a drawn plot of the Pebble Hill cemetery and from the cemetery itself. See also Marriage Record 1826 To 1837. Book A, 37, Ordinary's Office, Thomas County, and *ibid.*, 1839 To 1865, Book B, 38. See General Book B, 1837 To 1843, Ordinary's Office, 120, 146.

such time as her stepdaughter married or Martha Evans died. Johnson also named fellow Thomas countians Ewen McLean (also spelled MacLean), Thomas E. Blackshear, Michael Young, Thomas Jones, Mitchell B. Jones, Lott Warren, and Duncan Ray as trustees for Julia Ann and her child or children if she married. Everything not willed to Martha Evans went to Julia Ann, although Johnson specified that his property was not to be used to pay the debts of her future husband. If Julia Ann died unmarried and without children the planter's possessions would go to his sister Barbara Thomas, her children, and their "issue" (Johnson designated Pebble Hill for his niece Cynthia McLean and her children, with the remainder to be divided among Barbara's other children and their children).[5]

Whether drawing his will was some chilly premonition or the practical act of a practical man, probably the latter, Johnson had entered the prime of his life when in his mid-fifties he died on November 6, 1847. Managing Pebble Hill then became the responsibility of his widow Martha Evans and his daughter Julia Ann. From the time that Johnson settled at Pebble Hill until his death, his biography and the development of his plantation were, in many ways, also the story of Thomas County.

Johnson's Land Acquisitions. Johnson was still living in Pulaski County when he made the first purchase of land in what would become Thomas County. In November 1820, he paid John Garner $500 for the 250 acres of Lot 207, Eighteenth District, Early County.[6] Lot 207 bordered on present day Grady County. Immediately south of Lot 207 lay Lot 234, and Johnson added this land to his holdings in 1822 when he bought it from George Clifton for $500.[7]

---

[5]1845-1849 Returns, Book D, 116-118, Ordinary's Office, Thomas County.

[6]Deed Record Book A, Decatur County, 81, Decatur County Courthouse, Office of the Clerk of the Superior Court, Bainbridge, Georgia.

[7]Deed Record Book A, Decatur County, 84.

In 1822 Johnson made two additional land purchases. They came in January shortly after the lots were acquired by the initial owners. Lots 295 and 296 (both in present southwest Grady County and bordering on Decatur County) lay originally in Early County's Eighteenth District and comprised 250 acres each.

Still listed as a resident of Pulaski County, Johnson obtained Lot 296 from Anne Sanders. Perhaps she was a widow eligible for the land under the terms of the lottery law.

Securing Lot 295 was more involved. One Caleb Ethridge of Baldwin County drew the land in the 1820 lottery. He probably had little desire to leave the pleasant life that centered around Milledgeville for the wilderness of Southwest Georgia. In any case, in April 1821, Ethridge sold his land to Christopher McRae of Pulaski County. On January 13, 1822, Johnson bought Lot 295 from McRae, paying him $500. Before the month was out Johnson sold both lots to his brother-in-law, Josiah Everitt, another Pulaski County citizen. Everitt paid Johnson $500 for each of the lots. Assuming that Johnson paid $500 to Anne Sanders, undoubtedly the case, he had bought and sold 500 acres of land without making a penny's profit. Several months later, in September, Everitt sold lots 295 and 296 to Edward Blackshear, another prominent early settler who had migrated from Pulaski County. The transfer to Blackshear was made for $1,000, which meant that, like Johnson, Everitt made no money from the transaction.[8]

It is difficult—in view of the fact that Johnson both bought land (frequently) and sold land (less frequently)—to place strict or static geographical boundaries on Pebble Hill. When he drew his will in 1843, Johnson specifically mentioned three land lots: 246 (on which his home was constructed),

---

[8]Deed Record Book A-1, Thomas County, 76, 77, 77-78, 78-79; Deed Record Book A, Thomas County, 192-194, 194-196, 196-197.

247, which lay directly east of 246, and 275, immediately south of 246. The inference can be made that these lots of 250 acres each, all located in the Eighteenth District of what had been Early County, and all grouped together, constituted the heart of Pebble Hill. The plantation expanded from these 750 acres.

Johnson obtained Lot 247 and Lot 246 in 1825. His excellent eye for land and the inability of an owner to pay his taxes combined to produce Lot 247 for Johnson. In May in a *Fieri Facias* against one Thomas Combs, who for one reason or another had not paid his property assessment, Johnson was the highest bidder in a public auction. He paid $12. At the same time and in a similar transaction he bid $8 for Lot 6, Nineteenth District, Decatur County. Since no one offered more money, Johnson picked up this additional land for a minimum fee.[9]

As the site for his home, Johnson selected Lot 246. Without doubt the 250 acres appealed to him; the water was pure and plentiful and the undulating terrain of rich soil promised good crops. Magnolias, giant live oaks, dogwoods, beeches, hickories, crabapple, holly, and pine trees were abundant. The lot had been surveyed on November 15, 1819, by a crew no doubt appreciative that the summer heat was gone and the danger from snakes had lessened. In any case, the chief surveyor was Samuel W. Pearman. He was assisted by chains carriers Thomas Lea and Hezekial Wood and by James Marr, the marker or axeman.[10]

Lot 246 was originally granted to Seaborn Jones of Greene County, Georgia, on September 20, 1821.[11] Jones kept the prop-

---

[9]Deed Record Book A, Decatur County, 146-147.

[10]Original Field Notes, Eighteenth District, Original Early County, 1819, Surveyor General Department, Department of Archives and History, Atlanta, Georgia.

[11]Grant Book, Early County, District 17-18, GDAH.

erty without developing it and on November 28, 1824, sold it to John Lamar for $100. By the time of the sale Jones had moved to Bibb County.[12] Lamar, who was also from Bibb, held the lot less than a year. He sold it (at a profit of $50 for himself) to Thomas Jefferson Johnson on June 9, 1825, for $150.[13]

At this time Johnson moved to his new land. Picking out a desirable building site on Lot 246, he constructed the first dwelling on Pebble Hill.

Johnson's acquisition of Lot 275 was more complicated and came as the result of two purchases. The first occurred December 31, 1832, when he bought an estimated 98 acres from John B. Lacy for $110.[14] The remaining 152 acres were not added until four years later. In December 1836, Johnson paid Lacy $1,000 and became sole owner of Lot 275.[15]

Lot 6, Nineteenth District, Decatur (formerly Early) that Johnson acquired for the bargain price of $8 in 1824, at the same time he obtained Lot 247, had an unusual history. Because there is no record of a sale, it can be assumed that he gave Lot 6 to his brother-in-law and sister, Josiah and Eleanor Everitt. The Everitts were unable to keep possession of the land, and Johnson obtained it (as well as all property on it including twelve slaves) for $500. He then turned the land back over to Josiah Everitt for $20—adding a protective stipulation that should some one attempt to garnish the land it would revert to him. Johnson acted as he did because "I entertain great love & affection for the wife of said Josiah Everitt who is my Sister and also for her children who are my nieces & nephews now residing with her and also for the good will

---

[12]Deed Record Book A, Decatur County, 148-149.
[13]*Ibid.*, 146-147.
[14]Deed Record Book D-1, Thomas County, 285.
[15]*Ibid.*, 111.

and respect which I entertain & bear unto the said Josiah Everitt . . . ."[16]

Born in North Carolina in 1776, Josiah Everitt moved to Georgia with his parents after the Revolutionary War. After living in various places, he moved to Pulaski County and became a surveyor. Residing in the Hartford area, he met and married Eleanor Johnson. They had six children. In the 1820's Josiah and Eleanor lived in Decatur County, and for a brief period ran a hotel in Tallahassee, Florida. Some time after Johnson turned Lot 6 over to Everitt in 1832, Eleanor died. She was buried in the cemetery at Pebble Hill. Everitt was not listed as the head of a household in 1840, but he remarried in 1841 and died the next year.[17]

By 1829, Johnson had been married two years and would become a father for the second time. His planting interests were continuing to expand, and he indulged his penchant for dealing in real estate. In that year he made both a purchase and a sale. He paid $150 for Lot 279, which contained 250 acres. Although the property was still in the Eighteenth District, it was located on the Spring Hill road several miles from Pebble Hill. Lot 279 had originally been drawn by George Robert but had passed into the hands of John Young of Houston County, Georgia. Thomas Jones, a local lawyer, acted as Young's agent and sold the land to Johnson. Also in 1829, Johnson sold Lot 32, Eighteenth District, to William Bryan for $125. When or how Johnson acquired Lot 32 is not clear.[18]

Johnson bought Lot 235 (presently part of Melrose plantation) in 1832. The property lay directly north of Pebble Hill and was a natural part of it. Edmond Law of Georgia's Baldwin

---

[16]Deed Record Book B, Decatur County, 313-332, 479-480.
[17]Everitt family material loaned by Mrs. May A. Walton.
[18]Deed Record Book O, Thomas County, 199.

and Henry counties was the original drawee. The land next became the temporary property of John Lamar of Henry County. Lamar never lived on his property and soon sold it to Johnson.[19]

To some degree Johnson was interested in acquiring land not immediately contiguous to Pebble Hill. His interest took actual form in December 1836, with the purchase of part of Lot 43. In November 1837, he bought all of Lot 4, directly adjacent to Lot 43. Both lots lay in the Thirteenth District of formerly Irwin County and contained 490 acres each. They were located a few miles directly south of Thomasville.

Charles Kingsley, who owned Lot 43, sold 300 acres of the best watered portion, the southeast, to Johnson for $2,500. The price itself indicated a rapid rise in the value of land. The lot's remaining 190 acres were occupied by a Captain Thomas Harvey (and were deeded to Kingsley and to Moses Daniel). The transaction with Johnson was sealed with the proper legal information and made final with Johnson's signature and Kingsley's mark.[20] Moses Daniel sold the 490 acres of Lot 4 to Johnson for $1,200.[21]

In 1842, Johnson acquired Lot 240, Eighteenth District, when the original owners failed to pay the required taxes. The land reverted to the state, and as the highest bidder at a public sale, Johnson became the owner.[22] In the spring of the same year, 1842, Johnson picked up two more tracts of land at public auction. He obtained Lot 4, Sixteenth District, Decatur County, for $20.25, and Lot 5, Nineteenth District, Decatur County for $20.[23]

---

[19]*Ibid.*, Book E, 229.
[20]*Ibid.*, Book D-1, 284, 187-188.
[21]*Ibid.*, 122.
[22]Grant Book Reverted Lots, Early-A, 131, GDAH.
[23]Deed Record Book E, Decatur County, 341-342.

At some point Johnson acquired a 250 acre tract of land— Lot 73, Twenty-third District, formerly Early County. Located in present day Grady County, the property adjoined the Florida boundary. Evidently Johnson considered it too far from Pebble Hill for him to look after, and in 1844, he sold it to B. D. Hall for $300.[24]

One of Johnson's most unusual real estate negotiations concerned Lot 285, Eighteenth District (presently a part of Sinkola plantation). In August 1844, John G. Browning and William Browning of Thomas County signed a promissory note to Johnson for $440.41. They were to repay the loan by October 1, and as security they offered Lot 285. In August the Brownings further secured their note by putting up a woman slave, Amy, aged 26.[25] The men were as good as their word (or security) and paid off the debt.

Then in November 1845, possibly early 1846, the Brownings formally sold Lot 285 to Johnson for $250. A month later Johnson sold Lot 285 to Rual Evans for $250.[26] The reasons for the transaction are as intriguing as they are unanswerable. Did Johnson suddenly need $250? It is highly unlikely that he did. He was far too expert a planner and too efficient for that. Had Evans tried unsuccessfully to buy the land from the Brownings, failed, and then persuaded Johnson to step in as a sort of middle man to effect the deal? Whatever the reason, Johnson made no profit from his purchases and resale.

Johnson made his last purchases of land in 1845. His acquisition came as a package arrangement and involved a vertical tier of lots adjacent to Pebble Hill. The land lies in present Grady County, and the three lots form part of the

---

[24]Deed Record Book D-2, Thomas County, 226; Book E, Thomas County, 229.
[25]*Ibid.*, Book D-2, 204, 208.
[26]*Ibid.*, Book E, 286-287.

boundary between that county and Thomas. The lots involved included 233 (presently part of Melrose plantation), 248 (presently part of Pebble Hill), and 273 (presently part of Pebble Hill). Johnson made the purchase in 1845 from Dr. William Holland and Emily (Emely) Thomas Holland. Emily was the daughter of Johnson's sister, Barbara Thomas. Johnson paid the Hollands $1,500 for 83 ¾ acres in Lot 233, 115 acres in Lot 248, and 125 acres in Lot 273. Agreeing to the sale in separate indentures were Barbara Thomas and Emily's sister, Evalina (Evelina) Thomas.[27]

Most of the plantations that emerged in Thomas County before the Civil War were of moderate size. Many might more accurately have been called farms. Planters purchased land lots, cleared and cultivated them, and if they prospered and were sufficiently ambitious, added to their holdings as time passed. Pebble Hill was an exception. Johnson would, with at least 3,000 acres, have been a planter by any standard in Georgia and the South.

The Main House. Pioneer settlers in Southwest Georgia lived in houses in keeping with their environment. The typical farmer and his family dwelled in a modest structure. Depending on his fortunes, a man added rooms to his house to accommodate the growth of his family. At some point it was not unusual for him to construct an entirely new residence.

It is not possible to state precisely when the first Pebble Hill home was built. Land Lot 246, the site, as already noted, came into Johnson's possession in 1825. In 1827 he married Jane W. Hadley, and it seems certain that about this time the house was built. According to several sources, the initial Pebble Hill (ultimately there would be three) was a two story house. After his wife Jane died in 1830, Johnson lived at his

---

[27]*Ibid.,* 406-408.

plantation caring for his family and for his business and farming operations. In 1839 he married Martha Evans Everett. The records of how Martha Evans furnished her house offer insight into the way of life of a planter's family in Southwest Georgia.

The setting for the home must have pleased both of Johnson's wives. Pebble Hill lay almost due south of Thomasville, and the drive to town, some six miles, was a pleasant one except in bad weather. The main house was set back some distance from the Tallahassee road and was approached through a lane of large oaks. Slave cabins, farm buildings, and the family cemetery were in the area.[28]

Although Pebble Hill was comfortable, it was far from being ostentatious. It was true that both wives furnished the house with more and better quality items than were found in typical Thomas County residences, yet the interior was not lavish and the exterior was not palatial. Practical, utilitarian are words more descriptive and accurate. Each of the bedrooms contained at least one "bed matress clothing & bedsted" (one was valued at $50, two others at $25 each, and three at $30 each; another, when included with "furniture" and three trunks, was valued at $40, and a cot and furniture were worth $22). Mrs. Martha Evans Johnson placed a toilet table and looking glass in two rooms, and in two others she positioned a wash stand, bowl, and pitcher.

In various rooms were to be found a rocking chair, a dozen cane bottom chairs, six "common" chairs, and three split bottom chairs. Pebble Hill had a set of mahogany dining tables valued at $30, a mahogany stand worth $6, and three pine tables whose combined value was $4. Another pine table was listed

---

[28]See Mitchell's "Sketch of Pebble Hill." As shown in the original surveyors' notes, Lot 246 was well wooded and watered.

as being worth fifty cents. Other pieces of furniture included a side board, a "lot" of kitchen furniture, two candle stands, a couch and covering, and a clock. Johnson himself relied on his own timepiece, a $15 silver watch. The most valuable item in Pebble Hill was a piano forte and cover, that, together with music books, was worth $350.

Placed about the house were a number of candle sticks with trays and snuffers (the most valuable pair were silver plated and worth $8), a secretary, and three trunks. The home was also furnished with various items of glassware, pitchers, flower pots, and Long's map of the United States. In the kitchen could be found a pair or steelyards, crockery, a set of knives and forks, two dozen silver spoons, numerous jars, tin buckets, wash pans, a water bucket, three bail buckets, and six covers for dishes.

Because hunting for food and pleasure were so popular, all male residents, and many females, of Thomas County were familiar with firearms from early childhood. The acquisition of his first gun was a significant event in the life of every young boy, and expert marksmanship was a mark of prestige. No exception to the rule, the owner of Pebble Hill possessed weapons and kept them in his home. Johnson had two double barreled shotguns, a rifle, and two revolvers—only one of his pistols had a case. Such a collection was hardly an arsenal and was by no means unusual. Perhaps more unique was that Johnson had twenty-seven books shelved in one room of Pebble Hill and ninety-six in another. Few men in the county could match his library.[29]

After Johnson died in November 1847, Martha Evans, as his widow, took over the estate. Her daughter, Julia Ann Johnson, remained at Pebble Hill also. In May 1849, Julia

---

[29]1845-1849 Returns, Thomas County, Book D, 154, Ordinary's Office.

Ann married John William Henry Mitchell (usually known as John W. H. or J. W. H. Mitchell), and after Martha Evans died in 1850, the young Mitchell couple became the owners of the plantation. At about this time Mitchell replaced the original two-storied home with a one-leveled structure.

The second Pebble Hill, built in the shape of an H, contained eight rooms and a kitchen. Six of the rooms were 16x16 feet and one was 16x20. The home featured a large hall. One tale contends that Mitchell modeled his home on one he had seen in Canada. In any case, if the floor plan was not unique, the quality of construction and the ability of its builder were. The frame structure was built by John Wind, a talented young English architect (and inventor and coffin maker as well).[30] Supposedly brought to Thomas County in the late 1830's by Jackson Jones Mash, a local planter and merchant, to build him a home, Wind had remained. Thomas Jones's Greenwood plantation, the Thomas County Courthouse, and various residences and public buildings were designed and built by Wind. Pebble Hill was characteristic of his work.[31] Apparently both owner and builder were pleased because Wind ran an advertisement in a Thomasville newspaper listing Mitchell as one of his satisfied customers.[32]

Added to several times, the second Pebble Hill would stand until 1934 when it was destroyed by fire. A new and third Pebble Hill was completed by the plantation's owner, Mrs. Kate Hanna Harvey, in 1936.

Farming Operations. As Johnson and others hewed their plantations from the pine wilderness of Southwest Georgia, they

---

[30]Notes in Hopkins Collection based on interviews with her father, H. W. H. Hopkins. Information also supplied in interviews between the author and Mrs. Parker Poe.

[31]Mitchell, "Sketch of Pebble Hill."

[32]Thomasville *Southern Enterprise*, January 7, 1861.

developed farming units that were remarkably self-sufficient. They were aided in their efforts by good soil: basically gray sandy loam with red clay subsoil (in some places there were yellow sandy clay formations).[33]

Pebble Hill produced not only "money" crops, but its own food, and in many cases—and out of necessity—products that in more settled areas could be purchased in stores. The county had no navigable rivers, roads were little more than rude trails slashed through the wiregrass, there was no railroad until 1861, and there was no major trading center in the vicinity (Savannah was 200 miles away). St. Marks and Newport, two port towns located on Florida's gulf coast some fifty or sixty miles distant from Thomas County, served as markets for planters and farmers to sell and ship their cotton. The two gulf towns' wholesale and general merchandise stores, such as those owned by Daniel Ladd of Newport, enjoyed considerable business from Johnson and others.

At best it was difficult and inconvenient to get to the Florida coast. Even after Thomasville developed its own stores and business establishments, the difficulty of going to town— and the limited selections once arrived of both luxuries and necessities—made it imperative for a farm unit to be as self-sustaining as possible. Pebble Hill was such a plantation.

Among Johnson's livestock were beasts of burden as well as animals used for food. In 1847 he had 75 head of hogs, as well as 29 additional swine classified as "meat hogs." Johnson's smokehouse groaned with 2,000 pounds of pork, an amount that did not include 70 pounds of bacon listed separately. Also on hand were 100 pounds of lard. The planter had 24 head of "stock cattle," and 90 head of sheep.

---

[33]*Prosperous Georgia The Ideal Home For All Classes* (Atlanta, 1900), 88.

Johnson's slaves plowed his fields with oxen, horses, and mules, although that last historic hybrid was not common in Southwest Georgia. In 1847 he owned two yoke of oxen; a mare mule named Pet; Mack, a black horse; Jack, a bobtailed pony; a grey horse named Luke; and Bill, a bay horse. Some of the horses were used primarily for riding. Johnson owned three saddles, one of them the side saddle variety designed for ladies. For pleasure and business trips he had a barouche, a four-wheeled carriage with the driver's seat in front, two double seats inside facing each other, and a folding top, and harness. Just before his death Johnson acquired a new barouche and two sets of harness worth $200.

Pebble Hill produced a variety of agricultural crops. Sugar cane, corn (which along with fodder was used for feed), and evidently, tobacco were grown. In 1847 Johnson had on hand six boxes of tobacco valued at $120, an amount strongly indicating that it was produced on the plantation.[34]

Cotton was a major crop, and Johnson was always interested in improving the quality and quantity of the staple. In 1839, his friend, Thomas Butler King, sent him from Monticello, Florida, twenty seeds of "the celebrated Alabama twin cotton which is held in the highest estimation in that state...."[35] In fact, the expensive seed sold for twenty-five cents each. Johnson made as much or more money from his Sea Island cotton as from the hardier and more common short staple upland variety. Although he produced fewer bales on fewer acres, market prices for Sea Island cotton in the 1830's and 1840's were excellent.

Johnson kept leather in large supply and used it to repair farming equipment and probably to make shoes for his slaves.

---

[34]1845-1849 Returns, Thomas County, Book D, 154, Ordinary's Office; see also Seward's "Sketch."

[35]Thomas Butler King to Thomas J. Johnson, January 30, 1839, Thomas Butler King papers, GDAH.

Sugar was manufactured on Pebble Hill, and the plantation was equipped with a sugar mill as well as various sugar boilers and skimmers. Several barrels were always kept in reserve. At one point Johnson erected an elaborate and costly sugar manufacturing establishment, but the lack of a large market and poor transportation facilities caused him to abandon sugar refining on a commercial basis.

The master of Pebble Hill had farming equipment that included assorted wagons, harnesses, ox carts, yokes, hoes, grubbing hoes, stills, plows and plow gear, hand mills, scythes and candles (fingerlike rods that were attached to the scythes for mowing grain), and log chains. Proficient in the use of the equipment on the plantation were the slaves.[36]

Even before leaving Pulaski County, Johnson was a slave owner. On one occasion he paid $850 for a slave woman and her two children.[37] He probably brought his slaves to Southwest Georgia, and it is certain that he acquired bondsmen once he arrived. As a man of business and wealth, Johnson loaned money on a wide scale and sometimes took slaves as security. In 1842 Elizabeth McKinnon secured a debt of $27 by giving Johnson a mortgage on her slave, Hannah. In the meantime the owner died and Johnson acquired Hannah from the McKinnon estate.[38] The next year, 1843, Johnson had a business dispute settled by a slave whom he never owned. He sued one Richard Von Brunt (or Brundt) to collect a debt. Von Brunt had departed the state leaving property behind, and when the Superior Court ruled in Johnson's favor the

---

[36]1845-1849 Returns, Thomas County, Book D, 150-154; see also Seward's "Sketch."

[37]Deed Record Book E, Pulaski County, Superior Clerk's Office, Hawkinsville, Georgia, 37-38.

[38]Minutes Thomas County Superior Court 1842—1845, May Term 1842, 39—41.

sheriff took Von Brunt's slave Ellen, sold her for $266, and turned the money over to Johnson.[39]

For the most part, Johnson acquired his slaves by purchase and by the natural increase of birth. In 1830 he had eleven male and ten female slaves. The number made him one of the county's largest planters and clearly indicates that a large part of Pebble Hill was under cultivation at an early time.[40] Johnson's ownership of slaves hardly made him unique. If cotton cultivation, the plantation system, and slavery became characteristic of ante-bellum Georgia, the same general pattern emerged in the state's Southwest region. In fact, in Thomas County the slaves increased faster than the white population, and by 1850 more than fifty per cent of the county's people were Negroes.[41]

When Johnson died his property in slaves amounted to twenty persons—a total placing him among twenty-nine persons in that category (36 planters in the county owned more slaves.)[42] Nine of Johnson's slaves were male and eleven were female. Of the males classified as men, the list included Prince, two bondsmen named Silas, John, and Washington. Enumerated as boys were Tom, Frank, and Anthony, while Henry was listed as a child. Of the females the women included two Hesters, Lucy, Marie, Hannah, Flora, Ellen (and her child, Hannah), and Phillis. Sarah was described as a girl and Ann as a child. The most valuable males were John and one of the Silases, each worth $700. Prince, despite his name, rated

---

[39]Minutes Thomas County Superior Court 1841-1846, Book B, May Term, 1843.

[40]Original Manuscript Census 1830, Thomas County, 22, GDAH.

[41]For the general picture see Roland H. Harper, "Development of Agriculture in Lower Georgia 1850 to 1860," *Georgia Historical Quarterly,* VI (June 1922), 97-121.

[42]Mss. Slave Census 1850, GDAH; Rogers, *Ante-Bellum Thomas County,* 68.

as the bottom man on the economic scale: $150. Of the women Lucy was valued at only $25, while Hester and Flora were worth $500 each.[43]

It is not possible to determine precisely how Johnson treated his slaves, but from what is known of the man, it is probable that he was a benevolent master. Johnson's character would lead one to such a speculation. A friend remarked of him that he was a "man of general intelligence and great volubility of speech. A man of great and good heart. His corn crib was always open to the poor."[44] The slaves on the plantation, although under the control of their master, had their own sense of justice. According to one story (undocumented but handed down and probably true), in the early days of Pebble Hill an Indian murdered a slave. The other slaves captured the Indian and hanged him to an oak tree on the plantation.[45]

The Post Civil War life of one of Johnson's slaves, Sarah, indicates her owner's disposition. Taking the name of her former master, she became Sarah Johnson and settled down in one of the houses at Pebble Hill. Affectionately known as Aunt Sarah, she remained there until her death sometime before World War I.

Sarah Johnson became locally known for her uncanny ability to grow flowers and locally famous for her ability to dance. She could, at the same time and no matter how frenetic the gyrations, dance and balance a pitcher on her head. In the post war decades she cared for a number of Mitchell family children. Around the turn of the century she became the benign, and stern when the occasion arose, nurse of young

---

[43]1845-1849 Returns, Thomas County, Book D, 154.
[44]Seward's "Sketch."
[45]Mitchell's "Sketch." The story is also recounted in various entries in the Hopkins Collection.

Miss Elisabeth Ireland (later Mrs. Parker Poe). Half a century later, in an interview, Mrs. Poe fondly recalled the wisdom of Sarah Johnson. Deeply imbedded in the white woman's memory were admonitions for living that the former slave had passed on. One of the nurse's favorite remarks preceded some anticipated performance by her charge. The black woman would tell the young girl, "I don't want any half way doings out of you." She also brought home the importance of considering one's fellow man by saying, "I don't want ever to hear you say 'who but me.' "[46]

It might be argued that Sarah Johnson remained at Pebble Hill because she had no other place to go, but it seems more likely that she remained there because she wanted to, because it was where her roots were. In any case, she was a vivid example of the plantation's continuity.

Pebble Hill was laboriously wrought from the forest by Johnson and his slaves. The owner relied heavily on cotton, but he also diversified. At his death he left behind a plantation that was well run, efficient, and profitable.

Johnson As A Man Of Business. Although serving occasionally on the Inferior and Superior courts, Johnson did so primarily out of a sense of duty. And despite being a town commissioner in 1832, he had little taste for politics. Perhaps Johnson's brief stint in the legislature soured him, but it is probable that he simply was too busy otherwise. Primarily, he was a planter. Secondarily, he was a man of business. Both occupations were interrelated, and both concerned the acquisition, disposition, and transaction of money—or its equivalent.

In 1842 the Grand Jury considered the depreciated state of Georgia's currency "a public evil of great magnitude." According to the Thomas County jurors, it was difficult to be

---

[46]Author's interview with Mrs. Parker Poe, June 6, 1972.

"deprived ... of a sound medium of circulation for the transaction of business."[47] As early as 1838 Johnson wrote a friend, "The people of this section of the country are now tied down to a depreciated Florida currency and they are in much need of a Bank and are determined if possible to have one."[48] Unfortunately, their determination went unrealized before the Civil War.

A citizen, writing in 1855, complained that Thomasville's business life was crippled without a bank. He lamented that "we are compelled to go to Tallahassee, a two days absence, to purchase a check of any kind, and pay in addition to the regular per cent on exchange, the sum of eight dollars passage money, besides fare."[49] In 1860, Edward Remington, who had become one of Thomasville's leading merchants, acted as agent for the Bank of Savannah and discounted bills of exchange and drafts at his store.[50] Finally, in 1861, the Cotton Planters Bank of Georgia was incorporated in Thomasville, but despite promising beginnings, it died with the Confederacy.[51]

Johnson transacted his banking business with such Florida institutions as the Merchant Bank of Magnolia, the Union Bank of Tallahassee, as well as with the Bank of Macon and institutions in New York City. In 1843 and 1844 the Union Bank sued Johnson over a dispute involving an unspecified amount of money. The Thomas County Superior Court ruled in favor of the planter. Unsatisfied, the bank appealed the ruling, but the court decided once again for Johnson.[52]

---

[47]Thomas County Superior Court Minutes 1842-1845, Grand Jury Presentments, November Term 1842, 75.

[48]Thomas J. Johnson to Thomas B. King, October 20, 1838, King papers.

[49]Thomasville *Southern Enterprise*, November 13, 1855.

[50]Thomasville *Wiregrass Reporter*, January 28, 1860.

[51]Rogers, *Ante-Bellum Thomas County*, 21-22.

[52]Minutes Superior Court 1842-1845, Thomas County, November Term, 1843, 148; May Term, 1844, 200, 203.

Because he was one of the county's wealthiest citizens, Johnson soon became a kind of unofficial banker. He loaned money to numerous citizens, usually at low rates of interest, with the loans secured by land or slaves. At the time of his death, Johnson held outstanding notes from a number of men. The notes ranged from a low of $4 to a high of $780.10. Although the specific amount of some notes was not recorded (precluding an exact calculation), it is no overstatement to conclude that money owed to Johnson easily amounted to around ten thousand dollars.[53]

Some examples of Johnson's financial transactions reveal him as a man who maintained his solvency by straight-forward methods devoid of shrewd bargaining. In the summer of 1838 John Bellami borrowed $1,296 from Johnson. Bellami must have expected a good crop year because he agreed to repay the money by January 1, 1839. As security Bellami put up two slaves: eighteen-year-old Aaron and William, twenty-four.[54] Johnson was equally willing to accept land as security. In August 1844, neighbors John G. Browning and William Browning secured a loan of $440.41. As security they relinquished to Johnson the 250 acres contained in land Lot 285 near Pebble Hill. A few days later they further verified their promissory notes by putting up Amy, a slave aged twenty-six.[55]

By the mid-1840's loans were more detailed and exacting. In 1845 Johnson joined several other prominent Thomas countians in making a loan to William Cunnell. The latter's indebtedness to Johnson amounted to $366.18. Cunnell offered his benefactors security in a variety of forms: two land lots in Thomasville, a Negro slave named Grace (about 55), two horses,

---

[53]1845-1849 Returns, Thomas County, Ordinary's Office, Book D, 150-154.

[54]*Ibid.*, Book D-1, 224-225.

[55]*Ibid.*, Book D-2, 204. See above section on Johnson's land for details of how he finally acquired land Lot 285.

a buggy and harness, a surrey and harness, seven cows and calves, twenty-five swine, a lot of corn and fodder, household and kitchen furniture, medical provisions and literary books, drugs and medicines, farming equipment, carpenter's tools, surgical and dental instruments, office furniture, and "the rest of my property."[56]

As a man of business, Johnson inevitably got involved in lawsuits. For the most part the legal difficulties concerned belated action by Johnson to collect debts. No doubt Johnson dropped some debts as uncollectable and, as acts of mercy, simply forgot about others. But he could not assume a gullible role and survive on the frontier of Southwest Georgia. The piney woods contained many types of people but few philanthropists. In his numerous cases, Johnson always won. The usual procedure was for him to make some kind of loan, and when the terms were not met (Johnson invariably gave the other party a generous amount of time to pay before instituting suit), he would appear before the Superior Court.

What became standard practice began in 1839 when Johnson sued Stephen Swain for debt and collected.[57] In 1841, he successfully sued to collect $34 and interest.[58] He was equally successful in three similar cases the next year.[59]

By far Johnson's most active period for involvement in litigation was 1844. During that year he successfully sought debt payment plus interest from Curtis Carroll, John White, Henry Heath, James F. Carter, Malcolm McAulay, and Kindred Braswell.[60] In 1845 (in a case continued from 1844), the court

---

[56]*Ibid.*, 327-329.

[57]Minutes Superior Court 1835-1840, November Term, 1839, 232.

[58]*Ibid.*, 1841, November Term, n.p.

[59]*Ibid.*, 1842-1845, November Term, 1472, 53; see *ibid.*, 1842, **May** Term, 6, 78-80.

[60]*Ibid.*, 1842-1845, May Term 1844, 212-213; November Term, 219, 221, 222, 225, 228. For the same cases see Book D Superior Court Records 1844, 200, 201-202, 202-203, 206-208, 226-227.

ordered first John Carlton and then Wright Carlton to pay Johnson $200 plus interest, and in another case decreed that William Hunnell should pay Johnson $300 and interest. That same year John S. Mash appealed, but to no avail. A court ordered payment of $273 to Johnson.[61]

The only lawsuit that indicated anything less than fairness on Johnson's part occurred in 1845. Johnson won in his attempt to force John S. Hart to complete payment plus interest on a loan first made in 1838. A number of other men had signed the original note which was made at sixteen per cent interest. The accepted rate of interest was eight per cent. In any event, although some of the money had been paid, Johnson sued for $1,509.63. The jury, taking into account partial payments and the high interest rate, awarded Johnson only $273.[62]

Other than the Hart case, Johnson was lenient in his business transactions. He understood the difficulties and pressures that he and, to a much larger extent, others faced, and he tempered his desire for economic gain. It is hardly to be doubted that he acquiesed when an acquaintance asked for an extension on a note: "The times are hard beyond parallel. It is truly a deed of charity for the creditor to extend the hand of indulgence to his debtor at this time. For my own part I have but little hope with the crop now planting to discharge all obligations."[63]

Johnson confined his economic ventures primarily to local matters: loaning money, buying and selling land (although he owned considerable property outside of Thomas County), and farming. Like other Thomas countians, however, he wanted to

---

[61]*Ibid.*, 1842-1845, May Term, 1945, 250, 300, 284. Declaration Book 1845-1865, 6-7.

[62]Book E, Superior Court Records, March Term, 1845, 54-55; Minutes Superior Court 1846-1854, May Term 1846, 6; Declaration Book 1845-1865, 54-55, lists Johnson as being awarded $373.

[63]G. W. Holland to Thomas J. Johnson, March 7, 1842, King papers.

see the area prosper. To this end he became active in promoting a railroad for the region.

The Atlantic and Gulf Railroad, tying Thomasville to Savannah and to its rival, Brunswick, on the Atlantic coast, was not opened until 1861. Yet beginning in the 1830's, Johnson made a major effort to secure a railroad connection for Thomas County. Under the leadership of Thomas Butler King, an influential planter who lived on St. Simons Island, the Brunswick and Florida Railroad Company was incorporated in 1835. The proposed line was to extend from Brunswick to "any point on the Florida line" deemed necessary.[64] Johnson, a friend of King, became treasurer of the line, serving from 1839—1841.[65] How Thomas County fitted in the scheme was made clear by an act passed in 1838. The law declared that the Brunswick and Florida was "authorized to construct one or more branch Rail Roads from their main trunk to the Florida line...."[66] The understanding was that a line would extend through Thomas County. Johnson not only bought property in Brunswick in anticipation of a future economic boom, he aided in underwriting the project and helped sell subscriptions.[67]

Despite all the efforts and good intentions, the road ran afoul of competition, waning interest, and financial distress. It was never constructed. That the area would have benefitted from the line—increased population, faster development, a more diversified economy—is doubtless true. Yet with hindsight, it seems likely that no profound changes would have occurred.

---

[64]*Acts of Georgia 1835*, 187-217. See also Edward M. Steel, Jr., *Thomas Butler King of Georgia* (Athens, 1964), 8-18.

[65]Mitchell, "Sketch of Pebble."

[66]*Acts of Georgia 1838*, 189-197; *ibid.*, 1837, 262.

[67]In King papers see A. L. King and Thomas Butler King Security Bond acknowledging Johnson in the amount of $30,000; see also *ibid.*, for Thomas Butler King to Thomas J. Johnson, February 14, 1839; A. L. King to Thomas J. Johnson, December 15, 1839.

Savannah and Brunswick would have become the main shipping points instead of St. Marks and Newport, Florida, for Thomas County planters. The line's lack of success was not due to Johnson, who worked hard to make it a reality.

Johnson was only fifty-four when he died on November 5, 1847, but he left behind an impressive list of accomplishments: politician, citizen-soldier, businessman, planter, pioneer settler in the wiregrass, author of the bill creating Thomas County, and co-founder of Thomasville. In Pebble Hill, his wife and daughter inherited an enduring legacy.

Chapter IV

BARBARA THOMAS

Thomas Jefferson Johnson's life was closely bound to that of his sister, Barbara Thomas. A discussion of her activities and her family is needed to make full the story of Pebble Hill. Barbara, whose name as often as not was spelled Barbary, married January 23, 1812, and her husband Richard Thomas died on July 17, 1822. Remaining in Pulaski County, she had to cope with ending one phase of her life and beginning a new one. During the ten and a half years of her marriage Barbara had six children (one died at age one and another at age two). As a widow with three daughters and a son to care for, her future seemed at best a bleak and desperate struggle. Once her brother had married and settled down at Pebble Hill, Barbara gathered her children and moved to Southwest Georgia in December 1827. Without doubt she was motivated by a desire to be with her kin, but as events demonstrated, she was never a burden to them.

Shortly after moving, Barbara began acquiring land in Thomas County; ultimately she assembled a moderate sized plantation of some 750 to 1000 acres. In the late summer of 1832, she bought Lot 248, Eighteenth District, which adjoined Pebble Hill. The purchase price was $370, and the property was obtained from William Mitchell, J. Spurlin, and Arthur Johnson.[1] In December of the same year the quiet but determined widow added 250 more acres to her holdings by the acquisition of Lot 273, directly south of Lot 248. One Zachariah Hopson was $300 richer as the result of the transaction, and both parties were apparently satisfied.[2]

---

[1] Deed Record Book B, Thomas County, 101; *ibid.*, B, 36.
[2] *Ibid.*, B, 139.

Barbara built her home on Lot 248 (it is likely that her brother helped with the expenses of construction), and set about caring for a family that included Cynthia Carolina, born November 2, 1812; Emily (Emely) Jane, born May 6, 1819; Evelina (Eveline) Elizabeth, born August 23, 1817; and James Decatur, born December 24, 1815. Her son married a woman named Elizabeth, and relations between Barbara and her daughter-in-law were cordial and close. After the young couple had two children, James died unexpectedly in 1841 at the age of twenty-five.

Combining hard work with an innate skill, Barbara Thomas became an excellent planter. In 1830 the capable woman owned 24 slaves (three more than her brother, Thomas Jefferson Johnson), and by 1840 she owned 37. Although sixty-one-years-old in 1850, and living alone, she did not let age deter her from managing a plantation of 27 slaves. Her real estate was worth $7,500. By 1860 she still owned 15 slaves, 8 of them males, who were quartered in four houses.[3] According to a friend, she provided "a home of peace and plenty." It was said of Barbara that "Her manner was rather reserved, a little exclusive, but her home was one of exceeding pleasantness and all who were well behaved were well received." Living on the frontier, she had to depend on her brother at Pebble Hill, but she also took her own precautions: "Having a number of slaves, she always kept her house well armed and maintained peace against all threatened aggressors."[4] The widow, who probably could shoot a gun as well as most men, displayed her spunk in other ways. In 1837 she refused to pay a charge that she considered unfair. P. Kere & Co., her creditor, sued to collect, but Barbara's defense was so persuasive that the Thomas County Superior Court ruled in her behalf.[5]

---

[3]Manuscript Census 1850, Slaves, 156; Population, 72; *ibid.*, 1860, Slaves, 51.

[4]Seward's "Sketch."

[5]Minutes Superior Court 1834-1845, June Term 1837, 103.

Her children grew up in Thomas County. On January 19, 1836, Cynthia married Ewen McLean.[6] A farmer-businessman, McLean had been unofficially adopted by Johnson, and he lived and worked at Pebble Hill. According to one story, Ewen and his brothers, Kenneth and Donald, arrived as immigrants from Scotland at St. Marks, Florida. They walked from the bustling little port north toward Thomasville and stopped off at Pebble Hill where Thomas Jefferson Johnson befriended them. He later helped establish them in business at Thomasville. Ewen and Cynthia moved to a home on Fletcher Street in Thomasville. There they would have six children and there Cynthia would pass more than half a century until her death in 1894. Ewen could not have made a better choice. Cynthia, always Johnson's favorite, was the most outstanding of the children. She was described as "cheerful, vivacious, intelligent, and witty, respected by all... for her goodness of heart and great purity of character."[7]

Emily married in 1843. Her husband was William P. Holland, a well known and prominent physician in the county.[8] Evelina seemed destined never to marry, but at the age of thirty-four she met and fell in love with Peyton Walden. Recently arrived in Thomas County with his brother John, Peyton was from Kentucky. He and Evelina married on February 19, 1852.[9] The marriage was brief and tragic, and from its end came an ultimate act of violence.

---

[6]Marriage Record 1826-1837, Thomas County, Book A. 188.

[7]Seward's "Sketch." Cynthia later moved to Thomasville. She died in 1894 and is buried in Laurel Hill Cemetery. See Thomasville *Weekly Times Enterprise*, January 20, 1894. Johnson was actually a silent partner in the business firm of the McLeans. This was revealed when Kenneth died in 1843. See Declaration Book D, Thomas County Superior Court, November Term 1843, 109-110.

[8]Marriage Record 1839-1865, Thomas County, Book B, 65.

[9]Marriage Record, Thomas County, Book E, 60.

Barbara added to the 500 acres she owned in Lots 248 and 273. In February 1839, her son-in-law Ewen McLean paid William Browning $450 for the 250 acres in Lot 287, Eighteenth District, and then immediately sold it to Barbara for $450.[10] The land lay one lot south and one lot east of Lot 273. She now had 750 acres. The estate, however, was partly in the name of her husband and her children. In 1843 Cynthia and Ewen sold Lot 233, Eighteenth District (250 acres located immediately north of Lot 248), to Barbara and her two other daughters. The purchase price was $300. Lot 233 had been part of the estate of Barbara's husband, Richard N. Thomas.[11]

The death of her son, James D. Thomas, in 1841 (he was buried in the Pebble Hill cemetery), forced another legal clarification of the estate. As James's administrators, Barbara, Emily, Evelina, along with Ewen McLean, paid to the deceased's agent $800 for the 750 acres in land lots 233, 248, and 273, Eighteenth District.[12] Then in 1843, Barbara sold to Evelina and Emily sixth-sevenths of Lot 248 (she probably retained the home for herself) for $3,000 and 200 acres of Lot 273 for $500.[13]

In 1844, Elizabeth J. Thomas, widow of Barbara's son, sold her mother-in-law Lot 37, which her husband had bought in 1839. James had paid $1,400 for the land which was located in the Fourteenth District close to the community of Glasgow. Lots in that district were 490 acres in size. Elizabeth had two children of her own and could have used more money, but her sale price was only $4. The reason, as Elizabeth explained in the official transaction, was because "of the maternal love and affection which I have and bear" for Mrs. Thomas.[14]

---

[10]Deed Record Book D-1, Thomas County, 389.
[11]*Ibid.*, E. 401.
[12]*Ibid.*, 408.
[13]*Ibid.*, 401.
[14]*Ibid.*, Book D-2, 258.

Barbara, who had no way to take care of the property, sold it in 1845 to Ewen McLean for $500.[15]

As has been previously described, Thomas Jefferson Johnson's last land transaction, a confusing one in 1845, involved Barbara and her daughters and lots 233, 248, and 273. Johnson bought parts of the lots from William and Emily Holland, with Barbara and Evelina agreeing in separate indentures, and paid them $1,500. It was further agreed that Lot 233 belonged to Barbara, Evelina, and William Holland (for Emily), and that lots 248 and 273 belonged to Evelina solely. In a curious act Johnson relinquished all claims for $1,600.[16] It is possible that Johnson had some claim on the land in the lots that he had not purchased outright and that the $1,600 represented a debt settlement. In any case, the transaction led to an arrangement that Barbara made in Evelina's behalf. In 1845, the same year as the negotiations with Johnson, Barbara deeded lots 248 and 273 to Evelina and also made an "Agreement" with her for Lot 233.[17] She obviously was trying to provide for her unmarried daughter.

Evelina was not without business ability of her own. In October 1850, she purchased Lot 272, Eighteenth District, which joined the land her mother had given her. Evelina paid John Walden $1,550 for the land.[18] In dealing with John she also met his brother and her future husband, Peyton.

The Walden brothers prospered in Thomas County, John more than Peyton. John soon became a prominent land owner, purchasing lots in Thomasville and several districts in the county. His heaviest investment was in the plantation domi-

---

[15]*Ibid.*, 376. Thomas had originally purchased the lot from James M. Vickers. See Deed Record Book C, Thomas County, 41.
[16]*Ibid.*, E, 407-408.
[17]*Ibid.*, 407.
[18]*Ibid.*, 563.

nated Eighteenth District. Between 1843 and 1851, John Walden bought in order seven Eighteenth District lots: 226, 212, 272, 215, 189, 214, and 188. He thus acquired 1,750 valuable acres. Peyton's activities were much more restricted. Perhaps he was a trader. At least in 1850 he sold A. T. MacIntyre, a prominent planter, four mules for $400. Peyton's sole purchase of land came in December 1853, when he paid John Smith $1,100 for Lot 286 in the Eighteenth District.[19]

At some point Peyton met Evelina and each was attracted to the other. In 1852 Evelina could hardly have looked forward to what seemed inevitable, a life of spinsterhood. She would soon be thirty-five. Then after she met and married Peyton, everything changed for the better, but the interlude of happiness proved brief. In the winter after her marriage, Evelina became seriously ill. Peyton summoned local doctors, including S. S. Adams and his brother-in-law William Holland. Despite their efforts, Evelina died on March 5, 1853.[20] She had been married for slightly more than a year.

Testimony revealed later that Peyton was dissatisfied with the care that William Holland had given his wife. Apparently he thought that better medical attention might have saved her. In any case, a serious estrangement developed between the men.

An incident in the spring of 1854 triggered their hostility. On horseback, Peyton encountered Holland driving a buggy down a country road. Peyton asked for the right of way but Holland refused to yield—it was explained later that he could not control his horse. Walden then passed the buggy and gave it a bump. At that, Holland struck him with a whip. Several days later Peyton and John were in Thomasville. During the morning they encountered Holland on the main street and

---

[19]*Ibid.*, Book F, 448. See receipt in A. T. MacIntyre papers, GDAH.
[20]Minutes 1854-1857 Thomas County Superior Court, November Term 1854, 8-20.

words were exchanged. When the doctor attempted to proceed up Broad Street, Walden knocked him down and a vigorous scuffle ensued. As witnesses rushed to separate the men, Walden managed to stagger to his feet. He had been stabbed in the stomach and arm with a small dirk. The knife belonged to Holland. The fight occurred on April 21, and despite efforts to save him, Peyton died the next night.[21]

When the case came before the grand jury in May three of the jurors were temporarily removed because of their close relationship to Holland. After a true bill was returned the indicted physician was released on bond. Three friends—William G. Ponder, Henry Wyche, and Thomes E. Blackshear—put up the required $20,000 bond.[22] The following November Holland was arraigned, pled not guilty, and the trial date was set. Thomas countians followed the proceedings closely. A packed court listened intently to the testimony. Witnesses related the differences between the two men and described the circumstances of the fatal fight. The jury retired and after due deliberation returned with its verdict. William Holland was found not guilty.[23]

Peyton Walden's estate, including all of lots 272, 273, 248, and 15 acres in Lot 233 and 328 acres in Lot 328, was sold at public auction in 1858. Walden had inherited all of the lots except 328 from Evelina. James L. Seward, a leading planter and politician in Thomas County, was the highest bidder at $11,876.75.[24]

Despite the tragedy of Evelina, Barbara persevered. In 1856 she provided for Emily by selling 100 acres of Lot 233 to

---

[21]*Ibid.*

[22]Minutes Thomas Superior Court 1846-1854. May Term 1854, 392, 401.

[23]*Ibid.*, November Term 1854, 422-423; Minutes Thomas County Superior Court 1854-1857, 8-20.

[24]Deed Record Book H, Thomas County, 441.

William Holland for only $5.[25] One year later Barbara came to the aid of Cynthia, whose husband Ewen had died in 1855, by "selling" lots 274 and 287, containing 500 acres and located south of Pebble Hill, to her for $5.[26] Cynthia, every bit the daughter of her mother, prospered and in 1860 owned 35 slaves.[27]

By 1860 Barbara had parceled out much of her land to her children, but she remained a successful farm operator in her own right. In that year she had five horses, three mules, two working oxen, twenty sheep, and sixty swine. On her 200 improved acres and 290 unimproved acres were produced 1,000 bushels of corn, 800 pounds of rice, and 13 bales of cotton, as well as peas, beans, sweet potatoes, cane sugar, and molasses. The cash value of her farm was $4,000.[28]

Barbara continued to live at her home until she died in 1862. She was buried in the Pebble Hill cemetery. The homestead was destroyed by fire in 1868, and in later years her property was called the McLean Place, although it more properly should have been called the Thomas Place.[29] Barbara clearly had the drive, persistence, and ability of her brother. She was an admirable woman.

---

[25]*Ibid.*, G, 337.

[26]*Ibid.*, A-M, 171.

[27]Manuscript Census 1860, Slaves, 28-29.

[28]Manuscript Census 1860, Agriculture, 8-9.

[29]Barbara died intestate and not until 1890 was A. T. MacIntyre, Jr., appointed as her administrator. See Minutes X, 103; Bond Book 1880-1913, I, 66; Oaths, 69-70; Book U, 202; Letters of Administration Book J, 4. All in Ordinary's Office. See also Thomasville *Times Enterprise,* January 20, 1894.

Chapter V

"COURTEOUS TO HIGH AND LOW": THE MITCHELLS

After the death of Thomas Jefferson Johnson, his widow, Martha Evans, and his daughter by his first wife, Julia Ann, managed Pebble Hill. The difficulties of such an operation were made lighter thanks to Ewen McLean, the husband of Cynthia Thomas. McLean became the primary executor of Johnson's last will and testament. Although able to collect only a portion of the debts owed the estate—Johnson himself would have been unable to—McLean was an efficient administrator who gave timely aid.[1]

Less than a year and a half after her father's death, Julia Ann married. On May 10, 1849, Inferior Court Justice and family friend Henry Wyche performed the simple ceremony that made her the wife of John William Henry Mitchell, Sr.[2] If the marriage, which took place shortly before Julia Ann's twentieth birthday, lacked ostentation, it was clearly attended by members of both families. J. W. H.'s brother, George W. Mitchell, was anxious to join the gold rush to California, but his father wrote him to "get rid of such foolish notions...." The young man was advised, "Your brother John is to be married on the tenth day next & I want you to come home at that time without fail...."[3]

The Mitchells were a part of the Clan Innes near Strathblane, Scotland, who migrated to Ulster, Ireland. From

[1]For reports of Ewen McLean's work see Book E, 1849-1852, 30-31; Book 2, 1837-1849, 160; Book 3, 1849-1854, 9, 12, 40. See also Mitchell, "Sketch of Pebble Hill." The official county documents are housed in the Ordinary's Office.

[2]Marriage Record 1839 To 1865, Thomas County, Book B, 189.

[3]Nathaniel Raines Mitchell to George W. Mitchell, March 9, 1849. Apparently the father thought his son was going to be married a month earlier than he actually did.

there they came to America and settled in Chester County, Pennsylvania. Next they moved south to Prince George County, Virginia, and still later, to Thomas County. These Mitchells— and still another distantly related Mitchell family—became important in Thomas County and Southwest Georgia. Unfortunately, Martha Evans Johnson shared the happiness of her step-daughter's marriage for less than a year. On February 8, 1850, the widow Johnson died and was buried in the Pebble Hill cemetery.[4]

In accordance with Johnson's will, the state reverted to the original trustees. Since Julia Ann was now married, Ewen McLean and the other trustees declined to accept their appointments. Julia Ann appeared before Judge Augustin H. Hansell and petitioned that her husband become the sole trustee. Judge Hansell agreed, and John W. H. Mitchell, Sr., assumed the position officially on May 31, 1851.[5] In 1855, following the death and interment at Pebble Hill of Ewen McLean, J. W. H. Mitchell (already the trustee) became the official administrator of Johnson's estate.[6]

John W. H., born April 8, 1828, was the son of Nathaniel Raines and Temperance Jordan Mitchell, pioneers in Thomas County. Nathaniel Raines (1788-1854) and Temperance Jordan (1792-1843) were married in 1806. They moved from Montgomery County, Georgia, to Thomas County in 1827. A descendant described the Mitchells as "Simple in their mode of living, conservative in opinions, valuing very highly their traditions of good citizenship, courteous to high and low, pitying those in distress or poverty...." Physically they were "all tall, broad and large-limbed people, and some of great weight. There were

---

[4]Family Bible Records; Pebble Hill cemetery headstone.
[5]Thomas County Superior Court Minutes 1846, 201-211. See especially Exhibit E.
[6]Book 4, 1854-1860, 190; Bond Book E, 1849-1859, 136. Both books are in the Ordinary's Office.

John W. H. Mitchell, Sr. (1828-1865)

many handsome men among them," and as for the females, "the Mitchell women have always been content with their womanliness to a rather unusual degree. They were good wives and mothers and were diligent housekeepers, looking upon idleness for themselves and daughters as a social disgrace." Honesty was also a characteristic since the descendant wrote, "I must add that vanity of an unusual degree would crop out among them occasionally; naturally enough though, for the men of the family esteemed beauty above all else."[7]

Nathaniel Raines Mitchell married a second time to Lucy Hill who was buried in the Pebble Hill Cemetery. After his death the elder Mitchell was buried beside Temperance at their home place on the Thomasville-Boston road. John W. H. and George W. Mitchell served as executors of their father's estate. John W. H. was an interesting, laconic young man. That he was direct and to the point was demonstrated in a letter to his father: "I am sorry to inform you that I have nothing of importance to communicate to you on this occasion."[7-A] Like many farmers, J. W. H. felt an attachment to the soil that was so strong it affected everything he did. Once he worked briefly in Macon, Georgia, but soon wrote home, "My health is better now than it has been for some time past but it is not like it was when I left the corn field. The corn field suits me better than any place."[8]

Julia Ann bore her husband five children: Jane Temperance, born April 5, 1850; Martha Josephine, born October 2, 1852;

---

[7]Letter written by Mrs. Sarah Clark of Dixie, Georgia, in 1905, and kindly supplied to the author by Mrs. Kenneth (Marie) Klein of Deerfield Beach, Florida.

[7-A]J. W. H. Mitchell to Nathaniel Raines Mitchell, August 18, 1845, Nathaniel Raines Mitchell papers, GDAH. For the elder Mitchell's estate see Thomasville *Southern Enterprise*, June 6, 1860.

[8]J. W. H. Mitchell to Nathaniel Raines Mitchell, Novembr 6, 1845, Mitchell papers, GDAH.

Nathaniel Raines, born December 13, 1854; Mary Elizabeth, born January 26, 1857; and J. W. H., Jr., born February 10, 1859.

Jane Temperance, who married John Munro Stevens of Walthourville in Liberty County, Georgia, lived a long life, dying in 1935. Her husband was the son of Henry M. Stevens who refugeed from Liberty County to Thomasville in 1863. Both Jane Temperance and her husband were buried in Laurel Hill Cemetery in Thomasville.

Martha Josephine, known as Mattie J, married Charles E. Stubbs of Bibb County, Georgia, on February 11, 1875. He died tragically on July 17, 1875, near Macon. Stubbs never saw his only child, a daughter who bore the unusual name of Charles Wesley and was born January 25, 1876. In a ceremony performed at Pebble Hill by A. Warner Clisby, a Presbyterian minister, Mattie J married again on January 15, 1889; her husband was James Munro of Scotland and England. They had a daughter, Mattie Bell, born February 8, 1890. James Munro died November 27, 1907, at Brooklyn, New York and was buried at Laurel Hill Cemetery. Mattie J died November 15, 1929, at Baldwin, Long Island, New York.

Young Nathaniel Raines Mitchell, named for his grandfather, was not yet three years old when he contracted an illness and died on April 22, 1857. He was buried at Pebble Hill cemetery. Despite the child's unfortunate and untimely death, it was an age of infant mortality, and J. W. H. and Julia Ann were fortunate in being able to raise four of their five children.

Mary Elizabeth, popularly called Bettie, married Archibald C. Davenport on December 2, 1875. The marriage took place at Pebble Hill and was performed by J. O. A. Cook, minister of the Thomasville Methodist church. Davenport, who became a prominent citizen, died on October 14, 1916, at his home in Thomasville.

John W. H., Jr., was first named for his maternal grandfather, Thomas Jefferson Johnson, but his name was changed to that of his father after the latter's death in 1865. It was fitting that J. W. H., Jr., whose son was born in 1894 and would be the last Mitchell born at Pebble Hill, named the boy Thomas Jefferson Mitchell. J. W. H., Jr., lived at Pebble Hill as a bachelor until 1892.

During the 1880's Alexander Anderson McFarlan, like many other Northerners, was attracted to Thomas County. By 1888, McFarlan, his son, and friends were winter guests of the Mitchells at Pebble Hill. Later, McFarlan bought a tract of land across the Tallahassee road from Pebble Hill. He began regular visits in the winter seasons to Thomasville from his home in Bayonne, New Jersey. McFarlan named his Thomas County winter home "Alpine Grove." When his daughter, Laura Isabel, visited him she met her neighbor, J. W. H. Mitchell, Jr., and the two young people fell in love. The local paper reported in the summer of 1892 that John was on an important mission to New Jersey: claiming Laura Isabel as his wife. They were married on August 9. Besides Thomas Jefferson Mitchell, the couple had two other children, Laura Margaret and Alexander McFarlan Mitchell. Both were born in Thomasville. J. W. H. Mitchell, Jr., and his wife were buried in Thomasville.[9]

All of these births and marriages and deaths, of course, lay in the future for John W. H. Mitchell, Sr., and Julia Ann as they began the management of Pebble Hill following their marriage in 1849. The decade of the 1850's was both pleasant

---

[9]Hopkins Collection notes; Mitchell, "Sketch of Pebble Hill." See also Thomasville *Times*, November 17, 1888; Thomasville *Daily Times Enterprise*, May 17, 1889; July 29, 1892; Marriage Record 1885 To 1889, Thomas County, Book K, 469.

and prosperous for the Mitchells. According to one story, Pebble Hill got its name during this period. Credit has been given to Jane Temperance. Julia Ann, meticulous about the upkeep of her home—inside and out—saw to it that the walks were swept clean. Despite her efforts, rocks and pebbles were always rolling down onto them. Young Jane Temperance remarked to her mother that they lived on "pebble hill," and the name stuck.[10]

In 1850, J. W. H. Mitchell was only twenty-three and Julia Ann was twenty-one (Jane Temperance was a small baby) as they began caring for Pebble Hill. During the early years of their marriage the Mitchells commissioned the locally popular and talented John Wind to replace the original Pebble Hill with a new one-storied home.

Young Mitchell was hard working and knew the value of a dollar. An example of his thriftiness was seen in 1845 when he agonized over purchasing a horse. He needed one but concluded, "A good work horse is worth from $75.00 to $80.00 which is too much these hard times."[11] In 1850 Mitchell made forty-eight bales of cotton and his personal estate was valued at $6,000. He owned thirty-seven slaves.[12]

Building on the work of Johnson, Mitchell developed Pebble Hill into a profitable and diversified plantation. In 1860 his livestock—including two horses, thirteen mules, fifteen milk cows, and two hundred and fifty swine—were valued at $4,000. The planter depended mainly on his hogs for meat, and the value of animals slaughtered in 1860 was $1,500. That year the plantation also produced an impressive variety of other crops: 1,000 bushels of peas and beans, 4,000 bushels of corn,

[10]Hopkins Collection notes; Mitchell, "Sketch of Pebble Hill."
[11]J. W. H. Mitchell to Nathaniel Raines Mitchell, September 27, 1845, Mitchell papers.
[12]Manuscript Census 1850, Slaves, 156-157.

71

and 1,500 bushels of Irish potatoes. Good use was made of the sugar cane crop in that two hundred gallons of molasses and two hogsheads (of one thousand pounds each) of sugar were manufactured. The sugar and syrup plus two hundred pounds of butter brought the value of home manufactures to $300. Even more unusual was the production of eight thousand bushels of rice. Although far removed from the rice belt of coastal Georgia, Mitchell applied methods of irrigation and was one of the county's largest rice planters.[13]

On the eve of the Civil War, Mitchell's family was large and growing, and while the census gave him the modest listing of "farmer," he owned twenty slaves and quartered them in five cabins. Five of his slaves were inherited from his father, Nathaniel Raines Mitchell, who died in 1854. By 1860 Mitchell's real estate, valued at $45,000, and his personal estate, valued at $60,670, easily put him among the top planters in Thomas County.[14]

The cautious Mitchell did not loan money in the manner of his celebrated father-in-law. Thomas County's court records scarcely mention his name. Exceptions occurred in 1855 and 1859. In the first case the Superior Court ruled in his favor in a dispute with one William P. Smith over $419.92. And in December 1859, Mitchell was awarded $1,455 plus interest in a debt case against Curtis Carroll. As executor or co-executor of several estates, including that of his father, Mitchell also went to court.[15]

---

[13]Manuscript Census 1860, Agriculture, 5-6.

[14]Manuscript Census 1860, Population 38; Slaves, 3; Thomas County Wills, 1850-1855, 73-74, Ordinary's Office.

[15]Writ Record of Superior Court, 1843-1848, Book H, December Term 1855, 299-300, Thomas County; Thomas County Superior Court Minutes 1854-1857, November Term 1855, 115; *ibid.*, 1858-1865, December Term, 185. For his role as executor see *ibid.*, 1854-1857, November Term 1855, 100; December Term 1856, 210; and *ibid.*, June Term 1856, 162; December Term 1856, 162; June Term 1857, 253; December Term 1857, 299.

Still, Mitchell was similar to Thomas Jefferson Johnson in one respect: he liked to deal in real estate. In one case he had no choice. It involved a dispute that went back to Johnson and involved land Lot 275, an important part of Pebble Hill. Johnson had acquired the lot from John B. Lacy in two separate purchases, one in 1832 and the other in 1836. As executor of Johnson's estate, Ewen McLean was sued by Lacy who asked payment of $1,077.34 or the return of the southern half of Lot 275. McLean died before the case came up, but when Mitchell took over in 1856, Lacy asked for a new trial. The state Supreme Court agreed and ordered a new trial with Lacy bearing the costs of taking the matter to the higher court. Ultimately, Lacy won, and in 1866 collected $1,200 and costs.[16]

Mitchell was much more successful in land negotiations of his own. In 1851 he made an excellent buy when he purchased land Lot 277 in the Eighteenth District. J.W.H. paid George Smith $75 for the 250 acres.[17] The fact that Smith lived in Carroll County, Georgia, and may not have known the value of the property possibly accounted for Mitchell's bargain. Mitchell also owned land, probably inherited, near Brunswick.[18]

In 1858 the planter obtained another 250 acres in the Eighteenth District by offering the highest bid at a sheriff's sale at the courthouse. Lot 286, which had been the property of the late Peyton Walden (as previously noted, at this same sale the bulk of Walden's estate was purchased by James L. Seward), became a part of Pebble Hill—at the realistic price of $1,175.[19]

---

[16]Thomas County Superior Court Minutes 1854-1857, May Term 1855, 35; December Term 1856, 199, 214-215; June Term 1857, 241; Thomas County Superior Court Minutes 1866-1869, June Term 1866, 19.

[17]Deed Record Book F, Thomas County, 33.

[18]J. M. Tison to John W. H. Mitchell, February 24, 1856, Nathaniel Raines Mitchell paper, GDAH.

[19]Deed Record Book H, Thomas County, 515.

As the Civil War approached, Mitchell further increased his holdings. In 1860 he paid John W. Lightfoot $1,500 for Lot 276, a 250 acre tract lying in the Eighteenth District. That same year he obtained 200 acres of Lot 43, Thirteenth District, by paying $800 to William McLendon and others.[20] Of the 950 acres that Mitchell purchased, 750 became a distinct part of Pebble Hill. The other 200 in the Thirteenth District joined Lot 4 that Thomas Jefferson Johnson had purchased in 1837. The only sale of land made by Mitchell was in 1858 when he received $800 from Norman McLeod for 290 acres in Lot 419, Thirteenth District. The property lay to the east in Brooks County.[21]

A deep affection obviously existed between J. W. H. and Julia Ann. When he had to leave on business Mitchell always took time to write his wife. Traveling by stage on Georgia roads was hardly a pleasure, and one trip Mitchell made in 1850 to Macon and Milledgeville provoked a letter of complaint but one that also revealed his sense of humor. He wrote his wife that "I suffered a good deal on the journey from the intense cold weather that issued after leaving home. We got along very well until we got to Albany. At that place I was compelled to take an outside seat, and I assure you that the cold rendered my seat very unhappy."[22]

Mitchell never held political office and was not particularly interested, or at least he was not involved, in the political controversies of the 1850's. He opposed secession in 1850, but flirted with the Know Nothing movement, and as the state and the South moved toward separation from the Union, Mitchell gave his loyalty to the new nation.[23]

[20]*Ibid.*, I, 31, 160.
[21]*Ibid.*, H, 619. It is not certain how Mitchell or Julia Ann came into possession of this property.
[22]J. W. H. Mitchell to Julia A. Mitchell, December 11, 1850, Thomas Butler King papers.
[23]Rogers, *Ante-Bellum Thomas County*, 115.

Thomas County was part of the 2nd Brigade, 13th Division of the Georgia Militia. The most important post was that of Major General, and it was held by Thomas E. Blackshear. After Blackshear moved to Texas, the position became open, and J. W. H. reluctantly agreed to seek election to the post. The vote was held in early April, 1861, and Mitchell was defeated by a candidate from another, more populous county. Thomas countians gave Mitchell a lopsided majority, although not enough citizens voted to elect him. But he did not mind, and as the Thomasville paper said, he "consented to become a candidate merely to gratify some of his friends. There is, therefore, no disappointment or regret on his part."[24]

As the turbulent 1860's began, sectional tensions increased as everything seemed to be dominated by politics and military preparations. Yet the Mitchells, like everyone else, had personal crises as well. J. W. H.'s brother and sister, both prominent in Thomas County, died in February 1861. Thomas G. Mitchell and Mrs. Ann Blackshear both died within hours of each other. J. W. H. and R. H. Hardaway became executors of Thomas G. Mitchell's estate.[25]

In 1861 various volunteer companies were formed in the county, and John W. H.'s contribution of $100 was among the largest donations. Julia Ann became active in working with the Duncanville Ladies' Soldiers' Relief Society.[26] Once war began Thomas County companies left periodically for the front and were absorbed into regular Confederate units. The county and Southwest Georgia became important in furnishing foodstuffs and other supplies to the Southern armies as the war wore on. Thomasville, the terminus for the Atlantic & Gulf

---

[24]Thomasville *Southern Enterprise*, April 10, 1861; see *ibid.*, February 27, 1861, and March 6, 1861, quoting Thomasville *Wiregrass Reporter*.
[25]Thomasville *Southern Enterprise*, February 27, 1861.
[26]*Ibid.*, May 15, October 16, 1861.

railroad and a direct link to Savannah, occupied a strategic point. Southwest Georgia became a vital breadbasket.

As a man in his early thirties Mitchell was highly eligible for service in the Confederate army. Yet he was a large planter and had the responsibility of caring for his family. Not surprisingly, Mitchell sent a substitute during the war's first years.[27] Georgia's controversial Civil War governor, Joseph E. Brown, created a State Militia that was, in effect, a private army which he used to help defend Georgia. Thomas County furnished three units to Brown's State Militia—Captain J. J. Ivey's Company C which became a part of the Twelfth Regiment; Captain T. N. Gandy's Company E, also part of the Twelfth Regiment; and Captain Benjamin Franklin Floyd's company, attached to the Third Regiment. In the spring of 1864 Henry C. Wayne, Adjutant General of Georgia, appointed Mitchell Adjutant of the county's Battalion of Militia. Mitchell also served as a sergeant in Captain Ivey's company.[28]

In the spring of 1864 as General William T. Sherman's blue clad troops moved south from Tennessee, Governor Brown called up the Georgia Militia to help defend Atlanta. J. W. H. was among the untrained and inexperienced soldiers who went to the front. The green trooper participated in the grim fighting around Atlanta, and was furloughed in September, 1864, only to join a fast diminishing command as it reassembled at Macon in October. It seems certain that Mitchell was involved in the defense of Savannah. After Sherman presented Savannah to President Abraham Lincoln as a Christmas present, Georgia and the Confederacy tottered toward collapse. Governor Brown

---

[27]Enrollment List 7th Senatorial District—Thomas, Colquitt, and Brooks counties—1864, GDAH.

[28]See Muster Roll Co. C. 12th Rgt., 4th Brigade (McCoy's) Georgia, GDAH; Georgia Adjutant General's Letter Book, Book 24, April 29-June 3, 1864, GDAH; William Warren Rogers, *Thomas County During The Civil War* (Tallahassee, 1964), 37-50.

withdrew his militia "Pets"—who had fought amazingly well despite their lack of training and equipment—from service in February 1865, and Mitchell returned to Pebble Hill.

Conditions at the plantations were disordered, and the amateur soldier was forced to begin the spring planting without the aid of an overseer. Besides the difficulties of obtaining woefully short seed and supplies, Mitchell had to supervise the work schedule and other activities of twenty-five slaves. Perhaps he was physically debilitated from his service with the Militia or perhaps he carelessly exposed himself. Whatever the case, Mitchell caught pneumonia, grew steadily worse, and died on March 5, 1865. Death came for him at the untimely age of thirty-seven. He was buried in Pebble Hill cemetery.[29]

Other people closely connected to Pebble Hill also died during the Civil War. As noted, Barbara Thomas, seventy-four-years-old and one of the county's unique women, died on January 9, 1862. She was soon joined in the family cemetery by two grandsons—the sons of Ewen and Cynthia McLean: Captain Richard James McLean of the Thomas County Rangers (Company E, 50th Georgia Volunteer Infantry), killed at the age of twenty-one on May 3, 1863, at the battle of Salem Church, Virginia; and John Ewen McLean, who had served as a sergeant in Company E of the 29th Georgia Volunteer Infantry, better known as the Ochlockonee Light Infantry. John Ewen survived the war but died on September 17, 1865. He was buried with Masonic rites and the Masons inserted a note in the local paper praising him. According to the Thomasville *Southern Enterprise,* he was a casualty of the war because "the disease which caused his death had its origin in his campaign exposures."[30]

[29]Mitchell, "Sketch of Pebble Hill."
[30]See Thomasville *Southern Enterprise,* September 20, 1865; see *ibid.,* October 11, 1865.

Because Thomas County was never invaded by Union troops, it served as an important haven for refugees from Savannah and other parts of Georgia fleeing Sherman's armies. Not until well after Lee's surrender at Appomattox in April did Yankee soldiers enter Thomasville, May 9, 1865. Even so, Pebble Hill offered an example of how the county had been practically stripped of young men and agricultural products. In 1866 Tax Receiver H. M. Chastain reported that the county's aggregate wealth was $2,946,581, a decline of almost $6,000,000 from what it had been when the Civil War began.[31] Having lost her husband, who died intestate, Julia Ann Mitchell faced the bitter and harsh years of Reconstruction.

Because John W. H. left no will, the Ordinary's Court made Julia Ann the administratrix of the estate. Court appointed appraisers listed two notes, one for $800 and one for $332.15, as due the estate, but in the unsettled times immediately after the surrender only the most flint hearted and persistent man, to say nothing of a widow, could have hoped to collect. The appraisers also listed valuable slave property—four of Pebble Hill's twenty-five chattels were valued each at $1,200, and none less than $100—that totaled $16,650. Yet the war ended slavery and the thirteenth amendment to the Constitution, ratified in December 1865, made the demise forever official.[32]

At some point Julia Ann developed heart disease, but she managed to keep affairs going. In the 1870 census she was classified as "keeping house." Her real estate was valved at $7,965 and her personal estate at $1,750. Residing with her were Martha Josephine (Mattie J), Mary Elizabeth, and John W. H., Jr. Also living at Pebble Hill were Temperence Brinson,

---

[31]Ibid., August 1865; see also Rogers, *Thomas County During The Civil War*, 102 and *passim*.

[32]See Inventory And Appraisement, F, 1847 To 1867, Thomas County, 339-342; Minutes Thomas County, 1860-188?, I, 374; Court Docket 1854-1868, H, Thomas County Court of Ordinary, 369. All in Ordinary's Office.

a twenty-three-year-old girl, and a three-year-old boy, Robert G. Wheeler.[33] A widow with a plantation to run, bills to pay, and various children and dependents to support, Julia Ann struggled against the depression ridden 1870's.

Whether the times were good or bad, certain expenses were inevitable. One year Julia Ann's account at Samuel J. Cassels Drug Store came to $27.65. Among the items she had purchased were blue stone, Ayers Ague Cure, kerosene oil, a peck of potatoes, an extracting pencil, essence of ginger, spirits of camphor, chlorate of potash, quinine, a lamp chimney and wicks, paper, raisins, a toothbrush, Tuss's Pills, machine oil, Hosletter's Bitters, quick silver, mustard, alum, creosote, Bailey's Pills, and castor oil.[34]

In 1875 Julia Ann paid board for sixteen-year-old John W. H. Mitchell, Jr., at Thomasville's Fletcher Collegiate Institute in the amount of $200. Young Mitchell soon left school to help his mother operate Pebble Hill. Mary Elizabeth attended Young's Female College in Thomasville that year, and her expenses came to $262. At Pebble Hill there were monetary charges for clearing and fencing. Hands had to be paid to chop cotton, cut and shock oats, and to cover the gin house and barn. Plow stocks had to be bought, wood hauled, and fields plowed. Julia Ann paid $25 to buy and have installed 2,000 fence rails.[35]

Yet by spending sparingly for commercial fertilizers and by budgeting strictly, she paid off her debts. By 1875 the widow Mitchell was one of a small minority of Thomas countians with money in a vault: some $800 deposited with A. P. Wright & Company, newly founded and the county's only bank. In that year she and Mary Elizabeth located buyers for two

---

[33]Manuscript Census 1870, Population, 4.
[34]Thomas County Returns, 1875-1877, 234, Ordinary's Office.
[35]*Ibid.*, 233-234. See also Mitchell. "Sketch of Pebble Hill."

horses they had raised, and, in addition, fattened and sold sixty-three hogs.[36]

As a result of a lawsuit, whose ramifications are discussed below, Pebble Hill was broken up in the 1870's. Julia Ann retained the main house and in 1880 had living with her a widowed daughter, Mattie J, and the latter's four-year-old daughter, Charles Wesley Stubbs. Also living at Pebble Hill were young John W. H., Jr., who was classified as a "laborer," and twelve-year-old Robert Wheeler. Another daughter, Jane Temperence, and her husband, John Stevens (listed as a "laborer"), and John's mother and father, Henry and Elizabeth Stevens, resided at the plantation as well.[37]

With the passing of time Julia Ann grew steadily weaker and was confined almost completely to Pebble Hill. When her heart finally failed on January 21, 1881, death was not unexpected. Few women had had a fuller or a more demanding life: running a plantation, raising a family, experiencing and surviving a brutal war, persevering despite the loss of her husband. The Thomasville *Times* spoke of her as "one of the most estimable women in the county...."[38]

Pebble Hill's division came in 1876 when Thomasville lawyer Robert H. Hardaway brought suit as trustee against "Julia A. Mitchell et al" in the Thomas County Superior Court. It is not clear why the suit was brought. Perhaps the heirs, considering their mother's failing health, believed that a division made before her death would avoid family disputes and legal difficulties. Or perhaps Julia Ann declined, on request, to draw a will and acquiesced in having the court settle the estate. Whatever the reason, the suit was brought, and as a

---

[36]Butler [Alabama] *Choctaw Herald*, April 28, 1875, quoting H. E. C. in New York *Tribune*.

[37]Manuscript Census 1880, Population, 1-2.

[38]Thomasville *Times*, January 21, 1881.

result of the court's ruling, the land was divided among five parties: Julia Ann; Jane Temperence (Jennie T) Stevens; Mattie J Stubbs; Mary Elizabeth (Bettie) Davenport, who as a minor was represented by her guardian, K. T. McLean; and John W. H. Mitchell, Jr., also a minor and also represented by the same guardian, K. T. McLean.

Julia Ann was awarded Lot 246, the site of Pebble Hill (confusion arises here because the decree gave her only 125 of the lot's 250 acres but left the other 125 acres unaccounted for), valued at $1,200; the eastern half of Lot 247 (125 acres) valued at $500; Lot 234, worth $275; and Lot 235, worth $275. The cash value of her land, located entirely in the Eighteenth District, was $2,250.

Jane Temperence's land was also located in the Eighteenth District and included Lot 275 ($1,500), Lot 313 ($250), and the western half of Lot 247 (125 acres valued at $500). Her property was listed in cash value at $2,250.

Mattie J received widely scattered holdings. She got the south half of Lot 4, Thirteenth District (250 acres) valued at $2,000. In addition, Mattie J received the south half of Lot 240 (Eighteenth District, 125 acres, $50), Lot 250 in the Eleventh District of Wilkinson County, Georgia, which was valued at $100, Lot 28 in the First District of Irwin County, worth $50, Lot 562 in the First and Third districts of Cherokee County, worth $20, and Lot 342 in the Twenty-First District of Wilkinson County, worth $30. Like Jane Temperence and her mother, Mattie J's property was estimated in value at $2,250.

Bettie Davenport got the north half of Lot 4, Thirteenth District, worth $2,000; north half of Lot 240, Eighteenth District, $50; and Lot 44 in the Twenty-Sixth and Second districts of Cherokee County, Georgia, $20. She, too, received property whose cash valuation was $2,250.

John W. H. Mitchell, Jr., got land in the Eighteenth District. He was awarded Lot 276 ($1,100), Lot 279 ($150), Lot 208 ($1,000), for a total of $2,250.

The rents and crops on Lot 247 for 1876 were to go to Julia Ann. To pay off certain debts Hardaway sold Lot 43, Eighteenth District, for $3,800 and Lots 245, Eighteenth and Second districts Cherokee County, for $80, and Lot 1031, Fourteenth and First districts Cherokee County, for $40.[39]

The splitting of the estate in 1876, and the death of Julia Ann in 1881, meant the partial—but not complete and only temporary—end of Pebble Hill as it had been fashioned by Thomas Jefferson Johnson and carried on by John W. H. and Julia Ann Mitchell. Just as the plantation's prosperity in the 1840's and 1850's reflected life in the rest of Thomas County, so did its decline in the 1880's and 1890's mirror those stringent years.

---

[39]Minutes Thomas County Superior Court 1876, 128-129.
Footnotes for Chapter VI "Years Of Decline"

Chapter VI

YEARS OF DECLINE

The harsh decades of the late nineteenth century were years of paradox for the people of Thomas County. Black and white farmers shared the miseries common to their counterparts in the rest of Georgia and the South: an absence of capital, crushing taxes, soaring prices for fertilizer and the essentials of operating their farms, poor financial returns for their cotton and other agricultural products. Yet in the midst of grinding poverty the county's economy was measurably aided by the emergence and growth of Thomasville as a winter resort. The ownership and the function of Pebble Hill underwent a major change as a result of this development.

Beginning in the 1870's Northerners began coming to Thomas County seeking relief from Yankee winters; more specifically, the warm climate and the aromatic pine-scented air were allegedly helpful to those afflicted with pulmonary and bronchial diseases. Convinced that breathing the county's air would be medically beneficial, a belief not discouraged by local leaders, Midwesterners and Easterners with lung disorders came south to Thomasville.[1]

Numerous boarding houses and hotels, most notably the Mitchell House and the Piney Woods, were opened to accommodate the winter visitors. Gradually the seasonal guests discovered the county's hunting and fishing attractions, and Thomasville itself, with its fine hotels and influential guests, became a fashionable resort. By the late 1880's the town's winter season drew far more people who were physically well than invalids, although the ill continued to come. A gala and

---

[1]See William Warren Rogers, *Thomas County 1865-1900* (Tallahassee, 1973), especially chapters six and eleven through sixteen.

endless series of dances, balls—each luxury hotel had its own orchestra—parties, dinners, and hunts drew people back season after season. One year's newcomers became the next year's regulars.

The visitors ranged from persons of moderate means to those of great wealth. Guests in the latter category frequently shipped their horses and carriages to Thomasville for the winter, and the town's reputation as a glittering winter spa soon became national and international. A typical scene on Broad Street on a given Saturday in December revealed an incongruous mixture of town merchants, industrial tycoons, cracker farmers, retired millionaires, sharecroppers (white and black), politicians, writers, nationally known entertainers, local citizens, and foreigners. The air crackled with the commingling of soft Southern drawls, flat Midwestern twangs, and accents too sophisticated to pin down.

The area's climate, terrain, and wildlife were a combination that acted as a powerful magnet for sportsmen. Native sons and daughters—young and old and in between—fished, it seemed, every chance they got or could steal. They angled in quiet brown ponds, from the banks of dark lakes and lagoons (their waters blue-black from the acidic trunks and roots of cypress trees), from meandering streams, from somewhat wider creeks, and from the lazy Ochlocknee River. Hunting was even more important. Natives and visitors hunted deer, wildcats, bears, possums, squirrels, raccoons, alligators, and foxes. Such game birds as doves, all kinds of ducks, and wild turkeys were plentiful, but the bob white quail emerged as the favorite for hunters.

Once introduced to the hunting attractions, Northerners became enthusiastic participants. The visitors formed a kind of colony, although they never became an "exclusive" colony, and from the first, winter guests and local citizens mixed

84

socially and in business. Helping to bridge the gap between Northerners and locals were rollicking foxhunts. The foxhunts were noted for their pageantry, although they ended, as often as not, in a comedy of errors. In any case, Thomas countians became used to hearing the sound of a horn and seeing a large group of men and women, attired in formal habits, urging their mounts to follow a pack of hounds in scrambling and furious pursuit of a bushy tailed and wily fugitive.

Less strenuous and more popular, however, was the absorbing sport of hunting quail. Shooting clubs had been organized earlier, and various contests in marksmanship were close and highly competitive. But clay pigeons and glass balls paled when compared to the sport of hunting quail. The larger hotels bought country property which they set aside as hunting preserves for their patrons. The visitors themselves, escorted by local sportsmen, ranged across the county in search of the brown speckled game bird that challenged them as hunters and whose eating qualities were unrivaled.

Several Northerners, among them Dr. John T. Metcalfe of Cold Springs, New York, became so enamored of Thomas County that they invested in permanent residences. They also urged their friends to establish themselves in Thomas County. The initial purchases were town houses, but soon sportsmen began buying country estates and converting them into hunting preserves. Much of the county's land was no longer cultivated. The acreage, frequently mortgaged, on which annual taxes had to be paid, represented an economic burden in many instances. Gradually then, Northerners bought the property. Sometimes the outside investors built elaborate homes on their newly acquired property. When possible, however, the owners repaired the original residences. This would be the case with Pebble Hill. Even after Thomasville's hotels lost their popularity and closed—the allure of Florida's climate and beaches grew rapidly toward the century's end—Northerners continued to come to Thomas County every fall for the hunting season.

The county's active social life did not decline. Dinners, formal parties, and hunts were rotated from one plantation to the next. A number of plantations—Melrose, Elsoma, Greenwood—became showplaces. The new owners helped preserve the area with soil conservation, wildlife protection, and reforestation programs. They also furnished employment for many local citizens, both black and white. What happened was that Thomasville and Thomas County, despite having abundant economic problems, experienced their own version of a "Gilded Age." But such developments lay in the future. The residents at Pebble Hill and the people of Thomas County who were suffering through the 1880's would hardly have predicted such a turn of events.

It is difficult to document what particular land transaction signaled the break-up of Pebble Hill. After the Mitchell estate was divided in 1876 and after Julia Ann's death in 1881, her children fashioned their own lives, and the inevitable followed: they made various dispositions of their property. Unfortunately, the record of that distribution was not always clear.

Bettie Davenport, the fourth born child, had received an equal division of land. Yet none of her inheritance was a geographical part of Pebble Hill.

Jane Temperence Stevens had received Lot 275, the western half of Lot 247, both indisputable components of Pebble Hill, and Lot 313 in present day Grady County. There is no record of when or how Thomas Jefferson Johnson, John W. H. Mitchell, Sr., or Julia Ann obtained Lot 313, although it could be considered a part of Pebble Hill. What Jane Temperence did with her part of Lot 247 and Lot 313 is not certain, although at some point she sold them.

Jane Temperence's Lot 275 had a complex history. In February 1885, she sold it to James K. O. Sherwood of Queens County, New York, for $600. Regaining the property in 1889 from a mortgage company in Scotland, she immediately sold it to H. R. Cooke & Bros. Somehow she got the lot back again and sold it to R. A. Cooke in 1895. The deed was cancelled in 1902, and in that year she finally sold the land parcel designated 275 to Charles H. Thorne of Cook County, Illinois, for $1,600.[2] It thus becomes a matter of record that a part of Pebble Hill temporarily left the control of the Johnson and Mitchell family as early as 1885.

John W. H. Mitchell, Jr., had been awarded lots 276, 279, and 208. Lots 276 and 208 were integral parts of Pebble Hill. Although by the 1890's Mitchell's major property was Lot 276, the young bachelor apparently lived in the plantation home on Lot 246. By this time Pebble Hill had ceased to function as a productive, self-sustaining plantation.

Mitchell's Lot 276, which had been acquired by his father in 1860, was valued in 1889 at $1,250. That amount, taken together with the value of his household furniture and effects, livestock, tools, corn, cotton, and other crops, came to $2,115. Mitchell also acted as agent for Alexander A. McFarlan. The land, horses, and tools of McFarlan were valued at $2,225.[3]

Although the Thomas County Tax Digest listed McFarlan's land as Lot 297, it seems more probable that it was Lot 245. In any case, McFarlan had acquired a portion of Lot 245 from the Widow Lizzie Jones. As will be shown in Chapter VII, Dr. Samuel J. Jones refugeed to Thomasville from Liberty County during the Civil War. He purchased considerable land in the Eighteenth District, and after Jones died his widow

---

[2]See the following Deed Record Books of Thomas County: T, 639; WW, 148; Y, 292; DD, 321; KK, 77.

[3]Thomas County Tax Digest, 1890, n.p., Ordinary's Office.

sold McFarlan 75 acres in 1888 for $600. The sale came in the fall, and the following April Mrs. Jones sold McFarlan two more parcels of the lot—one of 57 acres and one of 44 1/2 acres for $710.[4] Lot 245 lay due east of Pebble Hill, but, historically, had never been a part of the plantation.

By 1890 much of the original Pebble Hill, including the residence, was owned by Mattie J, Julia Ann's second child. Mattie J had lost her first husband, Charles E. Stubbs, in 1875. After his death she and her child, Charles Wesley, lived at Pebble Hill. In the division of the estate in 1876 the lots Mattie J received were not part of the plantation nucleus. Yet after her mother died without leaving a will, Mattie J inherited, or in some manner was awarded, Julia Ann's property, namely Pebble Hill: lots 246, the 125 acres comprising the eastern half of 247, 234, and 235.

In 1889 she married James Munro of Scotland and England. The marriage ceremony was performed by Presbyterian minister A. M. Clisby and took place at Pebble Hill. Yet the couple did not live on the place.[5] Munro had business interests in New York, and he and Mattie J moved there.

John W. H. Mitchell, Jr., acted as agent for his sister's property. Her interests included lots 246, 247 (125 acres of it), 234, and 235, all located in the Eighteenth District, and Lot 4 (245 acres) in the Thirteenth District. Taken together, Mattie J's land was valued in 1890 at $6,000. There was only a minimum amount of farming: the value of horses and mules, tools, and other property only increased the total by $870.[6]

[4]Deed Record Book XX, Thomas County, 609, 653-654, 782.

[5]Thomas County Marriage Record 1885 To 1889, Book K, Ordinary's Office, 469.

[6]Thomas County Tax Digest 1890, n.p., Ordinary's Office. The Tax Digest incorrectly lists Mattie J as owning 125 acres in Lot 245. It should have read Lot 247.

Mitchell's Lot 276 was valued at $1,250 (total value of $1,765) in 1891; such statistics indicate that he engaged, if he engaged at all, in limited farming operations. Besides serving as a representative for a Northern seed firm, Mitchell acted as agent for his future father-in-law's property (probably Lot 245). He was in charge of land valued at $2,000 (total value $2,050). Mitchell was still the agent for Mattie J's land: lots and parts of lots 246, 247, 234, and 235 in the Eighteenth District and 4 in the Thirteenth District, valued at $6,000 for the land with a total valuation of $6,200. There was no farming.[7]

Meantime, A. A. McFarlan continued his interest in acquiring land. In 1889 he was party to a mortgage for $3,500 from Mattie J who had put up her four lots in the Eighteenth District for security. Then in 1892 McFarlan assigned the mortgage to his son, Horace J. McFarlan.[8] The property was still officially in Mattie J's name but her possession was tenuous.

In 1891 Mitchell's property bore the same evaluation as it had the previous year, and he paid taxes totaling $1.[9] By 1893 he valued his own property at $1,000, McFarlan's at $2,000, and Mattie J's at $6,000.[10] Mitchell's Lot 276 did not appear on the tax rolls for 1894, while McFarlan was taxed under his own name for 176 acres on Lot 247 (245?) valued at $200. But Mitchell was listed as agent for an unnamed person, unquestionably Mattie J, for the four lots in the Eighteenth District and one in the Thirteenth District. The lands were valued at $6,000.[11] In 1895, Mitchell was still serving

[7]*Ibid.*

[8]Mortgage Record J, 262, Circuit Clerk's Office; see also Mortgage Record M, 329.

[9]Thomas County Tax Digest 1891, n.p., Ordinary's Office.

[10]*Ibid.*, 1893.

[11]*Ibid.*, 1894.

as agent for these lands, valued at $4,480—their drop in value was explainable in terms of the hard economic times.[12]

Shortly after Christmas, on December 28, 1895, Mattie J, officially listed as residing in Kings County, New York, sold to Horace J. McFarlan, legal resident of Hudson County, New Jersey, her property in the Eighteenth District: lots 234, 235, 246, and the eastern half of 247, 875 acres in all.[13] The price was $1, and the next month the mortgage against her was cancelled.[14] Thus, in late 1895, for the first time a major portion of the land comprising Pebble Hill plantation was not owned by a direct descendant of Thomas Jefferson Johnson.

Mitchell continued as his sister's agent in 1896, although her holdings, valued at $1,000 had been reduced to 245 acres in Lot 4, Thirteenth District. Mitchell's own tax evaluation for unspecified property was $400. The same arrangement stood for 1897 and 1898 and the valuations had declined to $980 and $385.[15] In 1889 and again in 1900 Mitchell's estate was worth $405, but he was no longer an agent for Mattie J.[16]

John W. H. Mitchell, Jr., besides looking after the interests of his sister and McFarlan, also dealt with his own land. In 1876 the court had awarded him three lots: 207 (the northernmost lots of Pebble Hill, purchased by his grandfather in 1820), 276 (acquired by his father in 1860), and 279 (bought by Johnson in 1829, and although part of Pebble Hill, separated by Lot 278 which was never connected to the plantation). Other property that Mitchell sold was land that he had previously been given.

12*Ibid.*, 1895.

13Deed Record Book EE, Thomas County, 252-253.

14Mortgage Record M. 329, Circuit Clerk's Office. In February 1906, Mattie J sold 245 acres, Lot 4, Thirteenth District, to Roscoe Link of Thomas County for $2,500. See Deed Record Book RR, Thomas County, 303.

15Thomas County Tax Digest, 1896-1898, n.p. Ordinary's Office.

16*Ibid.*, 1899-1900.

Lot 43, Thirteenth District, 200 acres, was sold for him by his Administrator to John C. Parnell on January 4, 1876. Mitchell was only sixteen at the time.[17] On that same day, Moses Isaac bought young Mitchell's Lot 286, Thirteenth District, purchased by his father in 1858, although not a part of the 1876 settlement.[18]

In 1881 Moses Issac and C. Rheinauer purchased from Mitchell seventy acres of Lot 207, Eighteenth District, which he had received from the family division, and Lot 275, Eighteenth District, originally purchased by Johnson in 1836, but which was not part of the 1876 apportionment.[19] Both lots were regained by Mitchell at the end of the year when he bought them from Medicus Mallette.[20]

Mitchell's Lot 207 figured in two transactions in 1882. In January, A. P. Wright and Company took a mortgage on it, but the mortgage was cancelled.[21] Then in March, Moses Isaac purchased the lot.[22]

Having divested himself of Lot 207, Mitchell next sold his other two lots, 276 and 279. In 1883 he sold Lot 276 to Charles L. Flint,[23] and in 1885, Stephen G. Powell purchased Lot 279.[24] By 1887 Mitchell got Lot 276 back from Flint with the aid of a mortgage from the Georgia Loan and Trust Company.[25] He next sold Lot 276 in 1892 to Mrs. R. A. Cooke.[26]

---

[17] Deed Record Book V, Thomas County, 74.
[18] *Ibid.*, P, 670.
[19] *Ibid.*, Q, 632.
[20] *Ibid.*, R, 251.
[21] Mortgage Record EM, 735, Circuit Clerk's Office.
[22] Deed Record Book R, Thomas County, 253.
[23] *Ibid.*, S, 109.
[24] *Ibid.*, V, 692.
[25] Mortgage Record H-M, 315; Mortgage Record, I-M.
[26] Deed Record Book BB, Thomas County, 149.

As has been outlined, after Julia Ann died in 1881, her children gradually disposed of their holdings in Pebble Hill. The decline in agricultural profits, even an inability to break even, the stringency of the times, and personal interests that took them away from Thomas County were all contributing factors. The most dramatic moment in the end of Pebble Hill as a Johnson-Mitchell owned plantation came in 1895 when Mattie J transferred her ownership to Horace J. McFarlan.

Even though Pebble Hill appeared to have seen its most brilliant days, and even though it had gone through a piece-meal dismantlement, appearances were deceiving. In short order Pebble Hill would be restored and assume a new role and a new distinction.

Chapter VII

ELSOMA, MELROSE, AND THE NEW ERA

Among the first of the Northerners to discover Thomas County and to develop a plantation there was J. Wyman Jones, a wealthy businessman and the founder of Englewood, New Jersey. Jones, born May 2, 1822, died August 22, 1906, had a long and successful career. Among other contributions that he made to Thomas County, Jones purchased the James L. Seward property on the Monticello road. From that tract of land which he acquired in three separate purchases in 1888, 1889, and 1891, Jones fashioned a wooded park.[1] He stocked the park with a variety of birds and wild animals and ultimately, in 1895, transformed it into Glen Arven Country Club, one of the first golf courses in the nation.[2]

Jones also bought land southwest of Thomasville in the Eighteenth District. It was known as the MacIntyre place, after its early owner A. T. MacIntyre. The MacIntyre family, different members in different generations, made important contributions to Thomas County. Jones's purchase in 1888 of 510 acres lying off the Tallahassee road consisted of lots 192, 193, and ten acres of 194. He paid the then current owners, W. H. McCartney and W. P. Sherrod, $5,000 for the property.[3]

Salome Maria Hanna, whom Jones had married June 23, 1886, shared his enthusiasm for Thomas County. Born May 17, 1844 (died April 15, 1907), Salome was the daughter of Dr. Leonard Hanna and Samantha Maria Converse Hanna. From their base in Cleveland, Ohio, the Hanna family became prominent at both the state and national levels. When Salome

---

[1]Deed Record Book X, Thomas County, 254; see *ibid.*, **Y**, 494; **AA**, 336; **JJ**, 196. The property was Lot D, Thirteenth District.

[2]Rogers, *Thomas County 1865-1900*, 289-291.

[3]Deed Record Book AA, Thomas County, 564.

married Jones, her first husband, George Washington Chapin (born February 22, 1837), had been dead for two years. Salome had two children by her first marriage: Henry Hubbell Chapin (born December 5, 1869, died July 12, 1881) and Charles Merrill Chapin (born April 19, 1871, died December 31, 1932).[4]

The Hanna family has been traced back to the thirteenth century (the spelling then was Hannay). The well known Hannas owned the castle of Sorby in Galloway, Scotland. Most of the family migrated to Ireland in the seventeenth century. Robert, the son of Thomas and Elizabeth Hanna, was born in County Monaghan in 1753. In 1763 he and his parents became a part of the Scotch-Irish emigration to America when they moved to Pennsylvania. In January, during the memorable year of 1776, Robert married Catharine Jones of Chester County. Then in 1779 they moved to Virginia. The same year Robert and Catharine had a second son. They named him Benjamin. Although born in Campbell County, Virginia, Benjamin soon struck out for the West and settled in Ohio. There, in 1803, he married eighteen-year-old Rachel Dixon. The couple raised their family in the town of New Lisbon where Hanna opened a general store that developed into a successful wholesale and commission business. One of Benjamin and Rachel's thirteen children was Leonard (March 4, 1806—April 16, 1862). As a young man Leonard went East to school and graduated from the Rush Medical College in Philadelphia. Returning to Ohio, Dr. Hanna practiced medicine and surgery in New Lisbon. In 1835, he married Samantha Converse (April 3, 1813—April 16, 1897). A native of Randolph, Vermont, Samantha had come to Ohio with her parents in 1824. A riding accident curtailed Leonard's work as a physician, and he helped with the family business. In 1852 Leonard and

---

[4]*The Book of Benjamin Hanna His Children And Their Descendants* (Cleveland, 1936), 130. See also Charles Elmer Rice, *A History of the Hanna Family* (Damascus, 1903), 29.

his family moved to Cleveland where he opened the same type of business as his father.[5]

Salome was the first of the Hannas to come to Southwest Georgia. She and Jay Wyman made extensive renovations and converted their place into a handsome country residence. The house was painted, a new wing was added, and Jones named the plantation "Elsoma," a title derived from rearranging the letters in Salome. In the 1890s the Jones began what became an annual event: a Christmas party complete with tree and presents for the families of the people, white and black, who worked on the estate. In 1899 the children added to the "Christmas tree" festivities by singing songs and delivering recitations.[6]

Charles M. Chapin, Mrs. Jones's son by her previous marriage, was a sportsman and expert shot but was also plagued by bad health. In the 1880's young Chapin came south to Bainbridge, Georgia, for his health. Dissatisfied there, he and his tutor were about to return home when someone suggested that he go to nearby Thomasville. He did so, and like others before and after him, Chapin found Thomas County to his liking. After his mother and stepfather acquired Elsoma, Chapin's attraction grew, and he expressed interest in acquiring Elsoma for himself. Although flattered by the request, the Jones's told the twenty-year-old youth to find another place close by.

Taking their advice, Chapin made a major purchase in 1891 of 1,323 acres. The land, lying in the Eighteenth District, eventually became the basis of Melrose plantation and was

---

[5]Rice, *History of the Hanna Family*, 5-7, 15, 27-29; Herbert Croly, *Marcus Alonzo Hanna His Life And Work* (New York, 1923), 2-3, 5, 51.

[6]Thomasville *Times*, April 14, 1888; Thomasville Daily Times Enterprise, December 27, 1889.

Elsoma at the turn of the century

made up of lots 205, 206, 236, 237, 244, and seventy-three acres of 245. Chapin made a few additional purchases in Thomasville, including eighty-six acres in Lot 41, Thirteenth District.[7] When Chapin got married on May 19, 1894, at Hoboken, New Jersey, to Esther Maria (Lili) Lewis, he had Melrose plantation ready for his bride to see and visit.

Melrose had a significant history. It was first owned by Paul Coalson (Colson). Born in 1797 in Burke County, Georgia, Coalson graduated from Franklin College at Athens in 1824. During his last two years he read law, and shortly after graduating was admitted to the bar at Athens. In the spring of 1825 Coalson married Elizabeth G. Blackshear. Elizabeth, born March 15, 1805, was the daughter of Edward Blackshear. Her mother was Emily G. Mitchell, daughter of Thomas and sister of Richard and Nathaniel Raines Mitchell. Edward Blackshear and his family had moved from Montgomery County to Thomas County where he died in 1829. In 1826 Paul and Elizabeth Coalson joined the migration to Southwest Georgia, and he opened a law office in Thomasville. Noting the connection with the prominent Mitchells and Blackshears, a contemporary wrote, "By his marriage, Mr. Coalson secured a large family influence, which was of great advantage to him in the profession."[8]

Coalson was a brilliant young lawyer, but his career was cut short by his sudden death on March 23, 1830. He was only thirty-one. A fulsome tribute to his legal abilities maintained that no matter how large or small the case, "he was equally industrious, sanguine, and persevering. His was a temperament that could admit to labor and at the same time

---

[7]Deed Record Book AA, Thomas County, 740. See *ibid.*, MM, 210; VV, 407. Author's interview with Mrs. Parker Poe, May 15, 1974.

[8]Stephen F. Miller, *The Bench And Bar of Georgia* . . ., I (Philadelphia, 1858), 194.

indulge its lively propensities."[9] Coalson was buried on his plantation.

Later, in 1835, Elizabeth married her first cousin, Henry Wyche, another of the county's earliest settlers. Yet Wyche did not take over the Coalson property as a matter of course. In February 1836, he paid $2,800 to Thomas E. Blackshear, brother of Elizabeth and administrator for Paul Coalson, for the 750 acres in lots 205, 236, and 245 in the Eighteenth District. Wyche added to his property in 1837 by purchasing Lot 244 from John M. Curry for $300 and in 1839 by buying from Daniel Kornegay lots 206 and 237 for $3,000. The additional 750 acres also lay in the Eighteenth District. When Elizabeth died in 1853 she was buried in the family plot beside her first husband.[10]

Wyche remarried. His second wife was Artemisia (Artie) Lester, and Wyche continued living on the Coalson place until August 1862, when he sold it to William R. G. Gignilliat for $15,000. The price indicated wartime inflation, but it also meant that Wyche had built up a valuable estate. Wyche's new residence was in the Twenty-third District where he bought 875 acres from his former brother-in-law, Thomas E. Blackshear.[11]

The name of the new owner was a strange one to the people of Thomas County, but Gignilliat was well known in coastal Georgia and South Carolina. The Huguenot family had fled from France to Switzerland and had come to America early in the eighteenth century. Settling first in South Carolina, members of the family moved into Georgia and became identified with the early Scotch settlers in McIntosh County on

---

[9]*Ibid.*, 193; see also 201-202.
[10]Deed Record Book B, Thomas County, 414; see *ibid.*, D-1, 123-124, 312. See also notes in Hopkins Collection.
[11]Deed Record Book I, Thomas County, 469.

the coast. William R. G. (or William Robert) Gignilliat (December 10, 1814—January 19, 1882) was born at Ardoch, his father's plantation near Darien, the seat of government of McIntosh County. William Robert graduated from Franklin College at Athens in 1838, and that same year married a seventeen-year-old girl named Helen Mary Hart. A native of Liberty County, Georgia, Helen Mary was a member of an English family that had settled in New Jersey and Pennsylvania and later spread into the Carolinas and Georgia. Of a definite scientific bent, she studied at Athens, and it was there that she met William Robert.[12]

Returning to McIntosh County, Gignilliat became a leading rice producer at his Greenwood plantation. The couple became prominent members of the plantation aristocracy. They were able to hire tutors for their three sons and to spend the summers in the mountains away from the fevers of the low lying tidewater area. Early in the Civil War coastal Georgia became the object of forays by Union raders, and as a cotton and lumber port, Darien was a target. Gignilliat's three sons all served in the Confederate army. Then on June 17, 1862, Helen Mary died, and shortly afterwards, Gignilliat married Janet Elizabeth Slade. The danger of enemy attack made him decide to "refugee" to Thomas County. That his fears were well taken was seen in July 1863, when Federal troops burned the town of Darien.[13]

As the new owner of the Coalson-Wyche place, Gignilliat had his share of difficulties. Even so, the non-native proved to be an able planter who contributed important agricultural

---

[12]Clark Howell, *History Of Georgia*, IV (Chicago-Atlanta, 1926), 528-529; Robert Marson Myers (Editor), *The Children of Pride A True Story Of Georgia And The Civil War* (New Haven, 1972), 451, 473; *Catalogue of the Trustees, Officers and Alumni of the University of Georgia from 1785-1894* (Atlanta, 1894), 10.

[13]Howell, *History of Georgia*, IV, 528-529; Myers, *The Children of Pride*, 451, 473; T. Conn Bryan, *Confederate Georgia* (Athens, 1953), 74.

supplies to the Confederacy. In the fall of 1864, the Confederate government impressed 10,000 bushels of his corn, paying the refugee $2.25 a bushel. By 1865, Gignilliat, like other Thomas County planters and farmers, had to pay a "tax in kind." The law was enacted by the Confederate Congress and included such items as corn, Irish potatoes, peas and beans, molasses and sorghum, rice, and cotton.[14]

A victim himself, Gignilliat was sympathetic to the plight of other Georgians seeking protection from Northern armies. In December 1864, and into January 1865, a South Carolinian, who had close family ties in ,Georgia, Professor Joseph Le Conte executed a series of daring escapades. Too old for military duty, the determined Le Conte successfully brought his daughter, various relatives, and friends from Liberty County to Thomasville. Le Conte and Gignilliat had been college classmates, and William Robert welcomed his old friend to the sanctuary of Thomas County. Among the people whom Le Conte helped rescue from Sherman's forces were his cousin, Dr. Samuel J. Jones, and Jones's wife, Mary. Jones, who had graduated from Franklin College in 1856 and the Medical College of South Carolina at Charleston in 1858, practiced medicine in Liberty County until 1863. Then, even though he was suffering badly from asthma, Jones enlisted as a private in the Liberty Mounted Rangers. After serving as a nurse in a military hospital in Charleston, Jones returned home on sick leave. When the area was overrun the young doctor was so sick that the Northern soldiers had not taken him prisoner.[15]

---

[14]William R. G. Gignilliat papers in Hopkins Collection.

[15]Joseph Le Conte, '*Ware Sherman A Journal of Three Month's Experience in the Last Days of the Confederacy* (Berkley, 1937), 46-48. See also Earl Schenck Miers (Editor). *When The World Ended The Dairy Of Emma Le Conte* (New York, 1957), 5, 14; Josephine Bacon Martin (Editor), *Life On A Liberty County Plantation The Journal Of Cornelia Jones Pond* (Darien, 1974), 94, 113, 122-123; Myers, *The Children of Pride,* 1576; and Rogers, *Thomas County During the Civil War,* 92-95.

Le Conte's perilous journey with Jones was accomplished in part by putting the emaciated and weak physician on a club-footed mule (so useless the Federal troops had declined to confiscate it) and leading the animal until it dropped from exhaustion. Then Le Conte helped Jones struggle on by foot until they reached the village of Doctortown. From there they came southwest by train to Thomasville. When Le Conte sent his relatives north to Albany, Gignilliat loaned him a wagon. According to the professor, "Mr. Gignilliat [was] as true a Southern gentleman as ever lived...."[16]

For the remainder of the war Gignilliat continued to supply the Confederacy with farm produce. Even though he realized defeat was inevitable, Gignilliat did not object to the assessments. Yet he must have cursed his bad luck. For one thing, in February 1865, he had in his possession $20,000 in Confederate bills, $10,000 in Confederate bonds, and 27 shares of railroad stock—all of which would shortly be worthless. For another, on April 15, 1865, the planter, unaware that General Robert E. Lee had surrendered at Appomattox on April 9, turned over 191 pounds of extremely scarce "bacon" (sides, hams, and shoulders) to the Confederate government at Impressment Commissioner's prices.[17]

The planter was pardoned by President Andrew Johnson in November 1865, and resumed farming operations. His world—the Southern world—had been revolutionized. The Confederacy was dead, the slaves were free, and no one knew what the future held. Gignilliat had no choice other than to attempt to adjust to the new scheme of things, but he was assailed by problems. In 1866 the planter had two mules stolen—a bright sorrel horse mule and a dark cream mare mule. He

---

[16]Le Conte, *'Ware Sherman*, 53.
[17]Gignilliat papers.

vainly offered a reward of $50 for the recovery of both, $25 for the recovery of one.[18]

Like his neighbor Julia Mitchell at nearby Pebble Hill plantation, Gignilliat negotiated with the former slaves. His 1867 contract was typical of those entered into by other Thomas County planters. Drawn up in January and approved by Freedman's Bureau agent, W. T. Flanigan, the contract was signed by thirteen blacks—all of whom made their mark. Curiously enough, eight of the workers were women. Four of the former chattels had taken the surname Mitchell; two, Felder; two, Evans; four, Gignilliat. The thirteenth and only "full hand" was Martha Munger. The blacks were to perform their labors as squads or gangs. Those who fed themselves and furnished half their mule feed got one-half of the crop they grew and harvested. If the planter fed them—three pounds of meat and a peck of meal a week—they were entitled to one-third of their harvest. A laborer had to have the owner's permission to leave the farm under subject of a $1 fine to be collected at the end of the year and divided among the laborers of his or her squad. The freedmen agreed further to "obey all commands of the employer" and to keep the plantation in repair. Otherwise, he or she could be fined and forced to forfeit any share of the crop. Any animal injured and any property destroyed had to be paid for by the guilty party.[19]

Gignilliat kept the plantation—1,500 acres made up of lots 205, 206, 236, 237, 244, and 245—until January 1, 1869. At that time he sold it to the same Dr. Samuel J. Jones of Liberty County who had come to Thomasville at the end of the Civil War with Professor Le Conte. Jones decided to return to Thomas County, and bought the Coalson-Wyche

[18]Thomasville *Southern Enterprise*, May 13, 1866.
[19]Gignilliat papers.

place for the bargain price of $3,000. The decline in value of $12,000 in seven years was graphic indication of the hard times of Reconstruction. Even so, the besieged Gignilliat may have been willing to sell at any price.[20] It seems probable that he returned to McIntosh County. His second wife, Janet Elizabeth, bore him two daughters. Gignilliat died of heart disease at his summer residence in Marietta, Georgia, on January 19, 1882, and was buried beside his first wife in St. Andrew's Cemetery, Darien.[21]

Samuel John Jones, born in Liberty County on January 3, 1838, was one of six children of William and Mary Jane Roberts Jones. Samuel married Mary B. Hayes of Macon in 1859. They had four children (Maggie Lila, born in 1860 in Athens; two girls who died in infancy at Thomasville, one in 1867 and the other in 1877; and a son, George Orville, born in Thomasville in 1869 or 1870). Dr. Jones brought his parents with him, and they shared his home until their deaths in 1886. Mary, who at thirty-eight was the same age as her husband, died in Thomasville in 1877. The next year in Savannah, Jones was married again, this time to Mary Elizabeth Mueller. Stricken with dyptheria at the age of fifty-one, Jones died in 1889. Both he and his second wife were buried in Laurel Hill cemetery.[22]

After Jones's death his widow sold the plantation in 1891 to Charles M. Chapin for $10,000. Chapin's Melrose represented the original Coalson land plus what Wyche had added—except for those acres in Lot 245 previously mentioned as being bought by A. A. McFarland from the widow Jones.[23]

---

[20]Deed Record Book L, Thomas County, 229.

[21]Myers, *The Children of Pride*, 1528.

[22]See genealogical chart in Jones family Bible; copy of the chart in Hopkins Collection; Thomasville *Times*, January 19, 1889; Myers, *The Children of Pride*, 1576.

[23]Deed Record Book AA, Thomas County, 740.

Melrose in the late 1890s

In the meantime, Jay Wyman and Salome Jones sang the praises of Thomas County to their friends and were particularly concerned about interesting members of the Hanna family. Besides Salome, Leonard and Samantha Maria Hanna had six other children: Helen Gertrude, Marcus Alonzo, Howard Melville, Seville Samantha, Leonard Colton, and Lillian Converse.[24] Howard Melville, more than anyone else, was attracted by the appeals.

---

[24]*Book of Benjamin Hanna,* 130.

Howard Melville Hanna
(1840-1921), the first of his family to own Pebble Hill

Chapter VIII

CHANGES AND CONTINUITY: THE ENDURING LAND

By the last 1880's brothers Howard Melville, popularly known as Mel, and Mark, a gregarious, highly sociable man, both spent part of the winter season in Thomasville. Mark married Charlotte Augusta Rhodes in September 1864, and from an early business association with his father-in-law, Daniel P. Rhodes, eventually established M. A. Hanna & Co. With the aid of Mel, Mark won economic success, and in addition to his triumphs in the business world, became involved in the equally competitive world of politics. Besides his own role (he later served as United States Senator from Ohio), Hanna became the man who guided William McKinley's journey to the White House.

Ida Saxton McKinley, William's wife, was of fragile health, and in March 1895, Mark Hanna persuaded the then Ohio governor that a visit to Thomasville would be good for the ailing Mrs. McKinley. No doubt the climate of Thomas County aided Mrs. McKinley's physical health, and there is no question but that it aided her husband's political health.

It is well known that the visit was as much political as social or medical. In the informal atmosphere of the sun parlor in Mark Hanna's rented Dawson Street home McKinley conferred with leading Republicans from all over the South. Firming up their support as a result of the meetings, McKinley went on to win the Republican nomination in March 1896, and the Presidency the following November. McKinley returned once again to Thomasville as Mark Hanna's guest in March 1899.[1]

---

[1]For McKinley's visits to Thomasville see Rogers, *Thomas County, 1865-1900*, 331-344; Croly, *Marcus Alonzo Hanna*, 60.

Mark's brother, Mel, born January 23, 1840, was also an industrialist. Not inclined toward politics, Mel directed his talents toward finance and industry. A native of Cleveland, he was associated with the family business, but he also had connections with the original Standard Oil company and the American Tobacco company. Cultured and intellectually inclined, Mel was an excellent conversationalist. He was particularly informed about medicine, and his interests led him to give financial support to various hospitals including the City Hospital of Thomasville established in 1905. Mel was so successful in business that he was able to retire at the age of thirty-five. Mel and his wife, Catherine (Kate) Smith, whom he married on December 28, 1863, at Hartford, Connecticut, had six children: Helen Hanna, who died three days after being born; Bessie Hanna, who died at childbirth; Mary Gertrude Hanna; Kate Benedict Hanna; Howard Melville Hanna, Jr.; and Leonard Hanna, who died four months after his birth.[2]

Mel Hanna made his first purchase of land on November 13, 1896. At that time he paid his nephew, Charles M. Chapin, the token sum of $1 for the approximately 1,323 acres that made up Melrose. With the aid of William Miller, an unheralded landscape architect who did much to beautify Thomasville and Thomas County, Hanna made certain repairs on the property. The place was referred to locally as the "Jones plantation," doubtless because Samuel J. Jones had owned it before Chapin. In December 1896, Mel, his wife, and Howard Melville, Jr., stayed there for the first time. While the place was being made comfortable the Hannas were house guests of the Jones at Elsoma.[3] Hanna retained the name Melrose for his plantation.

---

[2]*Book of Benjamin Hanna*, 130; Thomasville *Semi-Weekly Times-Enterprise*, February 11, 1921.
[3]Deed Record Book FF, Thomas County, 31-32; Thomasville *Southern Enterprise*, November 21, December 5, 19, 27, 1896.

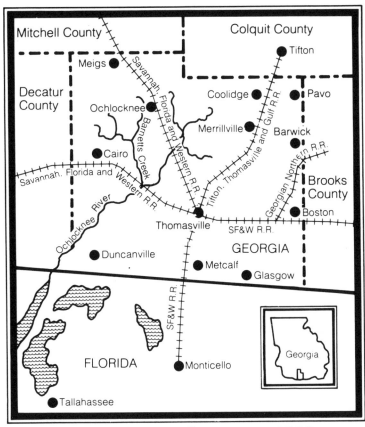

Thomas County, Georgia, in 1900

Having acquired Melrose, Mel Hanna decided to expand his holdings. Because the Pebble Hill land was adjacent, it was geographically logical to consider obtaining it, providing it was on the market. It was. As has been shown, the property had been transferred from Mattie J Munro to Horace J. McFarlan on December 28, 1895. McFarlan's proprietorshp was brief: he kept Pebble Hill less than two months. On February 20, 1896, he sold it to Judge H. W. Hopkins, a local sportsman, civic leader, and real estate man, for $2,000.[4]

Hopkins undoubtedly knew much of Pebble Hill's history and easily recognized its potential. Referring to the property as "the grand old plantation of the late John Mitchell," a Thomasville newspaper remarked that the "dwelling and the buildings are of the old southern style," and that they were "in a perfect state of preservation."[5] It was small wonder that the Hopkins Real Estate Agency planned to put it on the market. "This estate would be an ideal winter home and shooting preserve for one seeking a combination of climate and field sports," the newspaper concluded.[6]

After buying the property, Judge Hopkins held at least two dove shoots on Pebble Hill. One in March began at seven o'clock in the morning and ended a short time later at 8:30. The hunting party shot 245 doves. Pebble Hill was the scene of the last dove shoot of the season in April. Led by Judge Hopkins, a party of thirteen men and women began shooting at daylight, and bagged 325 doves, 2 quail, 1 wild turkey, and 1 rabbit.[7]

Hopkins owned Pebble Hill for slightly over six months, then he sold it to Mel Hanna for $3,000. The purchase included

---

[4]Deed Record Book EE, Thomas County, 314-315.
[5]Thomasville *Times Enterprise,* March 7, 1896.
[6]*Ibid.*
[7]*Ibid.,* March 21, April 4, 1896.

110

lots 246, 234, 235, and the eastern half of 247 (125 acres).[8] Pebble Hill, which had been in the Johnson-Mitchell family for the preceding fifty years, now passed to the Hanna family. The plantation's continuity has been maintained to the present day.

In 1898 Hanna purchased 44 1/2 acres of Lot 245 from Judge Hopkins for $356.[9] The Cleveland industrialist's next purchase was in 1900, when he paid S. L. Hayes $1,500 for Lot 207.[10] By the turn of the century Hanna had acquired Melrose, Pebble Hill, and other property in the Eighteenth District.[11] Mel decided to make some provision for his children Howard and Kate. On January 26, 1901, he gave his son, Howard Melville Hanna, Jr., "for and in consideration of the natural love and affection he has for [him]," plus $1, property in Thomas County amounting to approximately 2,367.5 acres. The only reservation was that "the grantor hereby reserves to himself a life estate in all of said property, hereby conveying only the remainder interest after the termination of said life estate."[12]

While he was turning land over to his son, Hanna also made a donation to Kate. Born on the day after Christmas in 1871, Kate Benedict Hanna was the fourth child. She was educated in private schools in Cleveland before going East to a girls' finishing school in Farmington, Connecticut. She then lived with her parents in Cleveland until May 2, 1894, when she married Robert Livingston Ireland of New York. Their national origins unmistakable, members of the Ireland

---

8 Deed Record Book FF, Thomas County, 524-525.

9 *Ibid.*, GG, 38.

10*Ibid.*, 266.

11Hanna's holdings included lots 205, 206, 236, 237, 244, 245 (117.5 acres north of the Tallahassee road), 234, 235, 246, 247 (125 acres), and 207.

12Deed Record Book ZZ, Thomas County, 450-451.

Kate Hanna Ireland with her children Elisabeth ("Pansy") and
Livingston - shown about the time she acquired Pebble Hill

family had migrated to New York in the eighteenth century. Ireland was the son of John B. and Adelia Duane Ireland. He was educated in Connecticut and New York and graduated from Yale University, class of 1890. Ireland settled in Cleveland, emerging as a successful businessman in hardware and later in shipbuilding. In 1903 he joined the Hanna Company, but he was also active in numerous other corporations.[13]

Kate and her husband moved to fashionable Prospect Street in Cleveland and soon had two children: Robert Livingston Ireland, Jr., born February 1, 1895 (married February 9, 1918, to Margaret Allen of New York); and Elisabeth Ireland, born October 31, 1897 (married April 5, 1946, to Parker Barrington Poe of Texas and New York). "Liv," as the son was called, and Margaret had four children: Louise, Robert Livingston, III, Melville, and Kate. Parker and Elisabeth, who inherited the nickname "Pansy" from an aunt, had no children.

Intelligent, able, and compassionate, Kate was of the same mould as Barbara Thomas and Julia Ann Mitchell. For $1 and because of his "natural love and affection," Hanna gave his daughter the eastern half of Lot 246 and "so much more thereof as may be on the southeast side of the Tallahassee Road as it runs through said lot." Mrs. Ireland's land contained the "frame dwelling house known as Pebble Hill."[14] Kate acquired the western half of Lot 246 and the eastern half of Lot 247 in 1911 as the result of a gift from her father and brother.[15]

---

[13]See typewritten "Historical and Biographical Sketch of the Ireland Family," compiled by the American Research Bureau, Washington, D.C., and "The Name And Family Of Ireland" compiled by the Media Research Bureau, Washington D.C., in private possession of Parker Poe, Thomasville. New York *Times*, February 18, 1928.

[14]Deed Record Book ZZ, Thomas County, 458.

[15]*Ibid.*, 451.

In the meantime, Mel continued to expand his holdings. K. T. McLean, son of Cynthia McLean and grandson of Barbara Thomas, had remained in Thomas County. He was a civic leader of Thomasville, having served among other offices, as mayor. By the mid-1880's, K. T. McLean, by marriage and inheritance, owned considerable family property in the Eighteenth District.[16] In the late 1890's he borrowed $3,029 from Mel Hanna, and put up as security five lots totaling 1,250 acres. When McLean paid his debts in 1902 the mortgage was cancelled.[17] A similar arrangement and cancellation was made that same year between Hanna and H. W. Hopkins regarding other property.[18]

In April 1902, Hanna added 800 acres to his property in the Eighteenth District. The acquisition was the result of a purchase from F. J. Winn.[19] The property became an enlargement of Melrose, but in the nineteenth century part of it belonged to a prominent planter named Joseph P. Neely. He came to Southwest Georgia from Washington County, and his wife, Elizabeth Jones Neely, was the sister of another pioneer, Tom Jones who owned Greenwood plantation. After Neely died in 1836, his widow married Dr. Thomas B. Winn. A widower himself for a year or more, Winn had married Mary Nelson Dickey in 1834. His wife had family ties to Fair Oaks, a plantation that will be shown as closely connected with Pebble Hill. Under Winn's ownership the plantation was called the "Home Place." Later, it was known as Winnstead. Besides

---

[16]On December 12, 1884, Kenneth T. (K. T.) and Elizabeth Katharine McLean obtained from Mrs. Cynthia C. McLean, Mary E., and Cynthia E. McLean lots 233, 248, 272, and 273, Eighteenth District, and 100 acres in Lot 101, Thirteenth District, Deed Record Book U, Thomas County, 23.

[17]*Ibid.*, V-M, 379-380. The lots were 247, 248, 273, 274, and 287.

[18]*Ibid.*, 380-381. The property concerned lots 382, 383, Eighteenth District; 25.9 of Lot 54, Thirteenth District; and lots 18 and 19, Twenty-third District. The note was for $2,000.

[19]The purchase price was $6,000 for lots 204, 196, 197, and 50 acres of 165.

his reputation as a physician and planter, Winn earned local fame for the large and delicious figs that he grew.[20]

The core of Winnstead was Lot 165. As early as 1902, Mary Gertrude Hanna, third child of Mel and Kate, had purchased 171 acres of it from Samuel L. Hayes for $2,500.[21] "Gertie" had married Coburn Haskell, a talented inventor, in 1895, and once in possession of Winnstead, completely rebuilt it around the foundations of the original square two-story residence.[22]

In the fall of 1902, Mel Hanna bought Lot 208, also in the Eighteenth District, from Mrs. Alabama T. Culpepper.[23] He obtained more land in the same district in the spring of 1904. On May 3, he paid K. T. McLean $1,250 for Lot 233.[24] The next day McLean sold Hanna land lots 248 and 272 for the token price of $10. Not unexpectedly, acquiring the 500 acres involved more than $10. Hanna supplied the money to McLean to pay off two debts amounting to $1,617.70.[25]

Having given his land in the Eighteenth District to his children in 1901, Hanna had now acquired an additional 1,300 acres. In March 1905, he again bestowed much of his land on his son. In return for $10 and the previous "life estate" reservation, Howard M. Hanna, Jr., received all of the 1,300 acres.[26] Although named for his father, young Hanna was

---

[20]Thomas County Marriage Record 1826 To 1837, Book A, 152; 1839-1865, Book B, 24; Thomas County Book of Wills 1856-1881, Book H, 83; *Rogers, Ante-Bellum Thomas County*, 55.

[21]Deed Record Book KK, Thomas County, 55.

[22]*Book Of Benjamin Hanna, family chart opposite 129;* author's interview with Gertrude Haskell Britton, April 16, 1979.

[23]Deed Record Book KK, Thomas County, 508. The purchase price was $1,600.

[24]*Ibid.*, NN, 187.

[25]*Ibid.*, OO, 254-255.

[26]*Ibid.*, NN, 524. The lots were 196, 197, 204, 208, 233, and 50 acres of 165.

called Howard to avoid confusion. There was little confusion about his business transactions. Howard Melville, Jr., became a spectacularly successful businessman. Beginning in 1908 and extending through the 1920s, Howard enlarged Melrose and bought other land as well. Much of the land was in the Eighteenth District, but many of the legal recordings were made in the courthouse at Cairo, county seat of newly created Grady which had been formed from Thomas and Decatur counties in 1905.[27]

Besides his own transactions, Howard received a final gift from his father in 1920: 1,817.5 acres in the Eighteenth District.[28] During his lifetime and in his will Howard, in turn, made provision for members of his family. A niece in an interview in 1979 remembered Howard's steadiness and his ability to assume responsibility. In 1930, he gave his sister Gertrude Haskell 343.4 acres in Grady County's Eighteenth District.[29]

Always generous to his children, Mel Hanna believed in keeping his property within the family circle. He made an exception in 1913 by selling 412.5 acres in five lots, Eighteenth District, to William H. Sage of New York for $45,000. The land was adjacent to Elsoma and was part of Boxhall plantation.[30] Lot 160, central to the land, had been bought first by Michael Young in 1835. In 1856 A. T. MacIntyre and his wife, America Young, bought it and the next year built Boxhall.

Mel and Kate Hanna died within two years of each other. In the spring of 1919 Kate died and left her estate to the

---

[27]*Ibid.*, TT, 442; ZZ, 459; 3-S, 551-552; 4-A, 525; Deed Record Book 10, Grady County, 66; 7, 553. For the creation of Grady County see *Acts of Georgia 1905*, 54-55.

[28]Deed Record Book 3-S, Thomas County, 388. The land included lots 205, 206, 207, 234, 235, 236, 237, 244, and 245 (117.56 acres).

[29]Deed Record Book 27, Grady County, 537.

[30]Deed Record Book 3-E, Thomas County, 46-47.

three surviving children: Howard, Kate, and Gertrude.[31] Mel died quietly at Melrose on February 8, 1921. Members of the eighty-one-year-old man's family were at his side, and, later, he was taken to Cleveland for burial.[32]

The Hanna family's interest in Southwest Georgia was extended at the turn of the century when still another of Leonard and Samantha's children acquired land in Thomas County. The fifth child, Seville Samantha, and Jay C. Morse, her second husband, bought land close to Elsoma and Melrose. Between 1900 and 1905 and as a result of a series of purchases, they acquired approximately 2,000 acres in the Thirteenth District.[33] The Morses named their plantation Inwood and became an integral part of Thomasville's winter colony.

While family members and relatives, especially her father and brother, were busy acquiring land, Kate Hanna Ireland had not been idle. In 1910 she added to the nucleus formed around Pebble Hill's homestead Lot 246 by paying K. T. McLean $6,875 for lots 248, 273, and the western half of 247, Eighteenth District.[34] Sticking to the same district in Thomas County and the same family, she bought 162.5 acres in Lot 274 in 1912.[35] The enterprising woman was especially active in 1915 when she not only leased 500 acres of land but made seven different outright purchases. The result was

---

[31]Thomas County Book of Wills 1915-1928, Book L, 159-161.

[32]*Ibid.*, 214-217; Thomasville *Semi-Weekly Times-Enterprise,* February 11, 1921.

[33]Seville Samantha was born March 30, 1846, died June 26, 1927. She was married on September 15, 1887, to James Pickands, born December 15, 1839, died July 14, 1896; she was married on January 11, 1899, to Jay C. Morse, born March 24, 1838, died August 22, 1906. See *Book Of Benjamin Hanna,* family chart opposite 129. For the land purchases see Deed Record Book II, Thomas County, 368; JJ, 71, 74, 205; LL, 469, 476; MM, 581; PP, 318, 320.

[34]Deed Record Book ZZ, Thomas County, 451; VV, 556.

[35]*Ibid.*, 3-C, 459; she paid K. T., M. E., and C. E. McLean $4,620.50 for the land.

117

Pebble Hill in the early 1900s after Howard Melville Hanna gave it to his daughter, Kate

that Pebble Hill was enlarged by some 1,645 acres.[36] All of the land lay in Grady County's Eighteenth District. The same district in Thomas County was the locale for 720 acres that she bought in 1920.[37] Throughout the 1920's and into the early 1930's—a time that saw her marriage end in divorce (in 1919) and during which she remarried—Kate remained active in civic affairs and in expending Pebble Hill. By various purchases during the period she acquired 4,167 acres, and like Thomas Jefferson Johnson, various Mitchells, and her own father, Kate almost never sold land.[38] In 1920 she made an exception when she sold her brother Howard 366 acres in Thomas County's Eighteenth District.[39]

Kate's second marriage was to Perry Williams Harvey. The son of Henry Allen and Mary Williams Harvey, he was born in Cleveland on May 10, 1869. Harvey attended Cleveland's Central High School and later enrolled in Yale University. There he played on the football team and graduated in 1891. He then became associated with the Hanna company. The wedding took place on February 12, 1923, in the living room at Pebble Hill. Friends and family were present, but there were no formal invitations or attendants. The ceremony was held at four in the afternoon, and after the Presbyterian minister, Dr. James D. Williamson, completed the ritual, there was a brief reception. According to a local paper, the couple

---

[36]*Ibid.*, VV, 566; Bond for Title, Book I, 89; Deed Record Book 10, Grady County, 57, 59, 61, 63, 81, 156.

[37]Deed Record Book 3-S, Thomas County, 493. The purchase price was $25,000 for lots 287, 315, 274 (83.5 acres), 316 (62.5 acres), and 314 (75 acres).

[38]After the divorce, Ireland married Mary Esther Wood of New York in 1920. In ill health and despondent, he committed suicide in New York on February 17, 1928. New York *Times*, February 18, 1928. Deed Record Book 10, Grady County, 197, 297, 375, 507; Book 25, 435-436; Book 27, 116, 386; Book 31, 19-20, 31, 53, 113.

[39]Deed Record Book 3-T, Thomas County, 285. The price was $5,000 for 314 (75 acres), 316 (Northwest .25), and 315.

then began a ten day wedding trip by taking "a late afternoon train, going west."[40]

In 1927 Kate made her most historically significant and interesting purchase. At that time she paid Mrs. Samuel Jones Mitchell $9,000 for half of Lot 250, Eighteenth District.[41] The gently sloping lot—studded with pines, oaks, and magnolias—contained Fair Oaks. The historic ante-bellum home had many ties to Pebble Hill. Located in Grady County about ten miles from Thomasville, between the Tallahassee and Cairo roads, Fair Oaks was originally owned by two men. In 1827—one hundred years before Kate acquired Fair Oaks—two brothers, Richard and Taylor H. Mitchell, bought the lot from William Lewis of Burke County, Georgia. The purchase price was $250, a dollar an acre. Richard achieved sole ownership on May 27, 1837, when he bought Taylor's share for $500.[42]

Born February 3, 1797, Richard Mitchell, a member of the state legislature when he lived in Pulaski County, would move from farmer to planter status and become a man of importance. He served Thomas County in both the House of Representatives and the Senate in the state legislature. His wife, Sophronia Dickey, whom he married on April 30, 1829, was born October 10, 1808, near Sumter, South Carolina. Her parents died and in 1826 she moved to Thomas County with her uncle Henry Atkinson. The Mitchells lived for one year with Richard's father and after that continuously at Fair Oaks for the rest of their lives. As the brother of Nathaniel Raines, Richard was the uncle of John W. H. Mitchell, Sr., of Pebble Hill plantation. Richard, a veteran of the War of 1812, was a man of firm convictions, and he nourished a hatred of

---

[40]Thomasville *Times-Enterprise Semi-Weekly*, February 13, 1923; Marriage Record 1921 To 1925, Thomas County, Book U, 351.
[41]Deed Record Book 31, Grady County, 19-20.
[42]Deed Record Book A-1. Thomas County, 250-251; D-1, 57-58.

Fair Oaks

121

Richard Mitchell
and his wife,
Saphronia Dickey,
owners of
Fair Oaks
in the nineteenth
century

England all his life. He was as well a hard worker, and the results were demonstrated by the expansion and improvement of his plantation. Mitchell also provided well for his family, which was large: he and Sophronia had nine children.[43]

Dying on February 12, 1856, Richard was buried in the family cemetery at Fair Oaks. According to local legend Mitchell made the explicit request that he be buried facing West. The indomitable Mitchell did not wish a geographical repose looking across three thousand miles toward his old enemies, the despised British.

Sophronia's son, Henry, built the first story of Fair Oaks for his mother soon after his father died. Supposedly there had been two earlier structures, each built to accommodate the growing Mitchell clan. The home's elegant architecture bears all the marks of John Wind's work. It would have been natural to have employed Wind's services, and it seems clear that he was the architect for Fair Oaks.

. Shortly before the Civil War began, another son, William Dickey (Bill Dick), added the second story, supposedly because he was bringing two friends home from college and wanted Fair Oaks to look more impressive. Bill Dick was said to have borrowed the money from John W. H. Mitchell, his uncle at Pebble Hill.

Sophronia lived on at Fair Oaks until her death on May 14, 1893. Although she was a profound Christian, Sophronia was not a member of a church. She was a woman of many friends and after her death the Thomasville paper reported, "Her kind, sympathetic, gentle and generous nature ever made her the object of admiration and devotion."[44]

---

[43]Fair Oaks and Mitchell Family Folder in Thomas County Historical Collection.

[44]Thomasville *Weekly Times Enterprise*, May 20, 1893.

Fair Oaks finally came into the possession of the youngest child, Amy Susan Mitchell McLean. Again, there was a connection with Pebble Hill. K. T. McLean, son of Cynthia and Ewen McLean and grandson of Barbara Thomas, was Amy Susan's husband. After Amy's death on March 9, 1919, Fair Oaks became the property of McLean, and following his death on February 4, 1924, there was confusion and litigation over title to the property. When McLean's sister, Cynthia Elizabeth, died intestate in 1924, the place was sold to Samuel Jones Mitchell and his wife, Martha Mallette Mitchell. Samuel was the great great grandson of Richard and Sophronia Mitchell. Shortly afterwards, in 1927, Kate Harvey bought the 125 acres from Samuel J. Mitchell's widow.[45]

Later, Kate's son Livingston Ireland inherited Fair Oaks. In 1940 he deeded it to Gertrude Haskell Britton, wife of Brigham Britton and daughter of Livingston's aunt, Gertrude Haskell. On moving from Cleveland, the Brittons took over a home that had no electricity and no bathrooms but plenty of ventilation from holes in the floor. They carefully restored and furnished the residence. Then in the acutely cold weather of 1962, a furnace pipe overheated, and the home was completely destroyed by fire. The Brittons rebuilt Fair Oaks with scrupulous attention to duplicating the original home in exact detail.[46]

Over the years Kate moulded Pebble Hill into one of America's most handsome estates. She increased the size of the house and added a garden and many plants and trees to complement the natural growth. Perry Williams Harvey shared his wife's love of nature and animals. He was part owner of

---

[45]See notes in Hopkins Collection as well as previously cited Deed Record Book 31, Grady County, 19-20.

[46]Deed Record Book 43, Grady County, 526; Author's interview with Gertrude Haskell Britton, April 16, 1979.

the Pastime Stables in Thomasville, and was an authority on standard-bred trotting horses. He was particularly interested in game birds, coordinating his avocation by working closely with the United States Biological Society. He and Kate developed Pebble Hill's natural setting into an excellent game preserve.[47]

Various other buildings were constructed including dairy barns whose architectual style was based on that of the University of Virginia. The architect was Abraham Garfield, son of the former President and a family friend and neighbor in Cleveland. Built in 1928, the red brick barns had an open space between the major structures that was planted in trees and outlined by a serpentine brick wall. At various places silos and turrets were coordinated in the barns and created the effect of a village in Normandy. Cottages and apartments were constructed as integral parts of the stable complex. At the same time, Garfield designed and completed twin gate-houses at the entrance to Pebble Hill and a wall around the family cemetery. With permission from the Mitchell family, Mrs. Harvey had the burying grounds repaired, more clearly marked, extended, and enclosed in the same brick and colonial style as the stables and gatehouses.[48]

White cottages built of wood dotted the grounds—they housed various workers and their families, some of whom spent their entire lives on the place. In 1929 Kate had built an exact replica of J. W. H. Mitchell's Pebble Hill. True in every detail to John Wind's original structure, the home was named Sugar Hill after an old sugar mill on the place and became a residence. Around 1902 Kate constructed on the

---

[47]*A Brief Biography Of Perry Williams Harvey* (Cleveland, 1930), 5-14.

[48]Author's interview with Michael Singletary, March 19, 1979; Author's interview with Mrs. Parker Poe, August 7, 1978; *Who's Who In America*, XVIII (Chicago, 1934), 934.

Part of the Jersey herd and one of the buildings in the cow barn complex. About 1930.

126

grounds a rustic two-room log cabin with a breezeway down the center. The cabin was first a playhouse and then a school for her children. Her daughter remembered starting school in the fall at Laurel School in Cleveland, remaining there until after Christmas, and then "Mother & ourselves & the household would pack up & leave for Thomasville." Part of the young girl's days would be spent in the log cabin where "I tutored every winter until May, when I would go back to Cleveland to join my class until I graduated from high school."[49]

An outstanding herd of Jersey cattle was developed at Pebble Hill. Grade Jerseys had long been on the plantation, but beginning in 1920, Mrs. Harvey purchased her first purebreds from Cherokee Farms at Thomasville. Then in 1922 she hired young Paul Sparrow to come to Pebble Hill as herdsman. The Harveys and Sparrow went to the Isle of Jersey and from that wind swept island off England's coast picked out stock. Other breeding stock was purchased in Canada. In 1928 William McPherson came to Pebble Hill to help supervise construction of the dairy barns, and in 1930 became manager of the plantation, a position he held until his death in 1946. Known as "Mr. Mac," he and Sparrow worked well together. The herd gained wide recognition—in 1930 one bull, Brampton Standard Sir, won 14 Grand Championships at major state fairs. Even more famous was Xenia's Sparkling Ivy, known more aptly as "Mother Superior," because of her remarkable progeny. Five of her sons won classification as Superior Sires and headed noted herds. "Mother Superior" earned numerous honors on her own, and her name and life span, October 12,

---

[49]Recollections of Mrs. Parker Poe. Written in pencil, these writings were set down in the late fall of 1978, and are in the private possession of Parker Poe.

1927—March 30, 1947, were engraved on a polished granite marker beside the dairy barns where she was buried.[50]

To manage the herd's activities a corporation, Pebble Hill Products, was created. More formal in name than in fact, the dairy was never strictly commercial. Its milk, buttermilk, cream, butter, cottage cheese and other products were dispensed from the County Store, a handsome building on the grounds. Most of the customers were employees—by a conservative estimate forty black and twenty white families lived on the plantation—who got the products at little expense. In 1938 the herd was dispersed, only to be built up again in the 1940's and finally dispersed in 1948 under the direction of Dr. Robert Hill, a veterinarian of Lexington, Kentucky. On both occasions the exceptional Jersey stock was made inexpensively available to the University of Georgia and various institutions. One of those benefitting was the School of the Ozarks, a self-help school in Arkansas that Kate and later, Pansy made contributions to.[51]

Like her father, Kate was interested in medicine, especially the broad area of providing medical attention for those who needed it. Early in the 1920's with the help of her daughter, she founded the Pebble Hill School and Visiting Nurse Association. The Association was supported by donations from various plantation owners, and primarily looked after the medical needs of their employees. Medical care was also the concern of William H. Watt, Sr., a businessman and civic leader of Thomasville. "Mr. Will" worked closely with Kate and Pansy; soon the nurses in their dark blue uniforms and collars—high, white, and stiff—became familiar figures. The Registered

---

[50]Author's interview with Louise Boland, April 10, 1979; James F. Deal, "History of Pebble Hill Plantation (Thomas County)," typescript. Deal's study of the Jerseys on Pebble Hill is scheduled to appear as part of a future book.

[51]*Ibid.*

Nurses were trained professionals; they varied in number from two to three, and the Association was an important adjunct and complement to county and state supported public health programs.[52]

The school part of the lengthy title had nothing to do with nursing. Public education in Georgia made progress during the 1920's but was seriously hurt by the depression years of the 1930's. In the segregated school system that existed at the time, black education was painfully inadequate. To care for the needs of black children, Mrs. Harvey established two schools on Pebble Hill, one on the Grady County part of the plantation and one at Pebble Hill proper, in Thomas County. Black teachers were hired and gave instruction in grades one through seven.[53]

Later, Pansy continued the work of the schools until the 1950's. In all of her humanitarian efforts Kate was supported by the Rev. Robb White, Jr., Rector of St. Thomas church in Thomasville from 1922 to 1938. Mrs. Harvey was also close friends with his wife, Laura Placadia Bridgers White. The Reverend White defied the stereotype of the Episcopal minister as a grave, reserved intellectual. Instead, he roamed around Thomas County caring for the indigent and comforting the sick, literally giving away everything that he had. Unpretentious, even disleveled (he washed his own shirts and underwear but never ironed them), the minister and Kate were a unique and formidable pair.[54]

Widely known for her hospitality and generosity, Kate, according to her son, Livingston, was a "wonderful sport," a

---

[52]Author's interview with Parker Poe, April 10, 1979; Author's interview with Louise Boland, April 10, 1979.

[53]*Ibid.;* Author's interview with Glen Sanford, April 16, 1979.

[54]Author's interview with Parker Poe, April 10, 1979; R. C. Balfour, Jr., *The History of St. Thomas Episcopal Church* (Tallahassee, 1968), 100-102.

woman considerably ahead of her time. Pebble Hill was a constant scene of guests arriving and departing. Mrs. Poe remembered John W. H. Mitchell's old home in the first decade of the twentieth century: "of course we had running water but oil lamps, hot water brought in cans for your bath, & each room with its fire place kept burning when cold."[55] Members of the family, relatives, and friends—many of them figures of national and international importance—wandered quietly around the plantation, hunted, rode, and enjoyed an active social season of dinner parties and various activities. As a wealthy person, Mrs. Harvey knew many affluent people, but she was no social snob. She had friends from all levels of society and numbered many Thomas countians, both blacks and whites, among her close acquaintances. Nor, despite her inherent kindness, was her behavior always saintlike. Glen Sanford, who went to work at Pebble Hill in 1921 and retired in 1978 after fifty-seven years, recalled how good she was, but added with a laugh, "until you made her mad."[56]

Tragedy came in the spring of 1932. Perry Williams Harvey had been suffering from heart disease for the previous four years and had been forced to curtail his activities. On May 24, his illness complicated by influenza, Harvey died at the plantation. The sixty-three-year-old man was buried in the extended section of the cemetery at Pebble Hill.[57]

In different form, tragedy came again in the winter of 1934. Thomas County had experienced a severe cold spell, and its citizens used every means at their disposal to keep warm. Pebble Hill had some ten or more house guests, and all of the fireplaces, including some not often utilized, were in operation.

[55]Recollections of Mrs. Parker Poe. Author's interview with Robert Livingston Ireland, Jr., May 15, 1979.

[56]Author's interview with Glen Sanford, April 16, 1979.

[57]Thomasville *Times-Enterprise*, May 24, 1932.
May 25, 1974.

After two o'clock on Tuesday afternoon, January 30, the family and their guests had barely begun luncheon when flames were discovered. The fire began in the attic, probably from defective bricks in a chimney, and the flames spread quickly through the main section.

The people inside took action—they soon were joined by workers and residents of Pebble Hill and nearby Melrose. The city of Thomasville sent a chemical engine and later a pumper to the scene, as hundreds of people in town came out. Observers remarked later that the heart pine wood created the blackest smoke they had ever seen. Fortunately, an efficient and hastily formed rescue organization of people saved most of the furniture, linens, clothing, and ornaments. The flames reached their height about 3:15; the front section was completely destroyed. The east wing of Pebble Hill was saved, but chimneys standing stark among charred rubble were all that remained of the rest.[58]

Construction was soon begun on another Pebble Hill. The large and comfortable home (including the east wing that escaped the fire) was an appealing expansion of the residence it replaced. It was completed in the winter of 1935-1936. Once again, Abraham Garfield was the architect, and his firm designed a three-story home of white brick that was Georgian in emphasis and featured eight columns across the main front section. Landscape architect Thelnyn Harrison of Cleveland designed the rose and camellia gardens and made other placements. Construction proceeded at a rapid pace largely because Mrs. Harvey employed so many workers. She was anxious to have the home replaced as rapidly as possible, but she also used the project to provide employment for numerous Thomas County citizens out of work because of the Great Depression.[59]

---

[58]*Ibid.;* February 2, 1934; author's interview with Mrs. Parker Poe, May 25, 1974.

[59]Author's interview with Michael Singletary, March 19, 1979; author's interview with Parker Poe, April 10, 1979.

Pebble Hill Plantation (Circa 1937), after completion of the new Main House

Changes and Continuity: The Enduring Land

By the mid-thirties Mrs. Harvey, although still vigorous, decided to make definite provisions for the future. In the summer of 1935 she divided her estate between her two children.[60] Mrs. Harvey developed pneumonia in the spring of 1936, and despite an emergency operation, died on May 15. Her good friend the Rev. Robb White, Jr., officiated at the burial in the Pebble Hill cemetery. "The death of this beneficient woman, greatly beloved and admired throughout this section," according to a Thomasville newspaper, was "a blow that will be reflected in many ways and among hundreds of the people here...." Considering Kate's life, her many charities and private donations, the paper's conclusion that she had a "noble character and a generous spirit," was a fitting one.[61]

---

[60]Deed Record Book 5-G, Thomas County, 359-371. Pansy was given 141 acres in Lot 274 and the western half of 246; Robert Livingston received 109 acres in Lot 274. For the major division of property see Deed Record Book 36, Grady County, 244-247.

[61]Thomasville *Semi-Weekly Times-Enterprise*, May 19, 1936.

Kate Hanna Harvey (1871-1936) She rebuilt Pebble Hill.

Chapter IX

"THESE LEGS DON'T WANT ME"

When Kate Harvey divided Pebble Hill, half went to Pansy and the other half went to her son Livingston Ireland. After Kate's death in 1936, the brother and sister agreed that Pansy would keep the Pebble Hill home and buildings.

Shortly after his mother's death, Livingston joined Allen Harvey, who was Perry's brother, and David S. Ingalls, a friend and fellow Clevelander, in forming the Grady County Shooting Syndicate. The syndicate continued until the 1960's. As his residence Ireland took Ring Oak, a duck shooting lodge, which bordered Lake Miccosukee just across the boundary in Florida. In 1940, Ingalls bought a side by side lodge and acreage at Ring Oak. Later, Ingalls greatly expanded his property there. In 1949, David's wife, Louise Harkness Ingalls, and Ireland jointly purchased a large plantation called Foshalee. It was west of Ring Oak, and, like that plantation, lay on the Florida side of the division with Georgia.

Liv's wife, Margaret Allen Ireland, died in 1961, and a few years later he married his first cousin, Louise Ireland Grimes. Other Hanna relatives continued to own property such as Melrose, Elsoma, Sinkola, and Fair Oaks in Thomas and Grady counties.

Elisabeth Ireland was known to her friends as Pansy and to an even wider circle of acquaintances as "Miss Pansy." She shared Kate's concern and love for people, animals, land, trees, flowers, lakes and streams, and hunting. Speaking in the spring of 1979, Thelma Lawyer, Mrs. Poe's maid for many years, said, "You can call her a lover of nature."[1] Pansy became one of the nation's leading sportswomen.

---

[1]Author's interview with Thelma Lawyer, April 16, 1979.
For Hanna properties in Florida see Clifton Paisley's informative *From Cotton To Quail . . . Leon County, Florida 1860-1967* (Gainesville, 1968) 91-93.

Born October 31, 1897, in the family's red brick home on Cleveland's Prospect Street, she soon moved with her parents to Lake Shore Boulevard in Bratenahl. The house was perched on a high bank overlooking Lake Erie, and nearby lived various family members, including Coburn and Gertrude Haskell, Howard and Claire Hanna, and other prominent Clevelanders. As a young girl Pansy occupied herself with swimming (she could dog paddle at ten months), boating, and caring for her animals. She played with stuffed animals, but soon learned to ride and owned her own pony by the time she was six. Often she roughhoused with Livingston and her cousins: "To amuse ourselves we swam or canoed on the big old lake, played ball, or maybe tag down in the Japanese garden, etc., etc." Brother and sister got along well but were not alike. Livingston remembered that "She walked her side of the street and I walked mine."[2]

Even before Kate acquired Pebble Hill in 1901, the Ireland family visited Melrose. "My earliest recollections down here," Mrs. Poe wrote in 1978, "were getting out of a pullman car and smelling the *wonderful* pine air, then driving out to grandmother's for a hearty breakfast & running over to Pebble Hill as quickly as possible. . . . We always lived in the woods & out in the country." At the age of four, "Mother would take me fox hunting, I riding my pony on a lead strap."[3]

There was also the matter of her formal education. Kate sent Pansy to Laurel school in Cleveland and provided a tutor, as has been discussed, for her in the log cabin at Pebble Hill. After high school Pansy went for two years to the Masters school, a finishing school at Dobbs' Ferry, New York.[4]

---

[2]Recollections of Mrs. Parker Poe. Author's interview with Robert Livingston, Jr., May 15, 1979.
[3]*Ibid.*
[4]*Ibid.* Author's interview with Parker Poe, April 10, 1979.

Young Pansy Poe and her pet dog

Pansy surpassed even her mother as an outdoors person and hunter. Practically living on a horse, she developed into an expert rider, showing jumpers on an international level. She was one of the few women polo players in the country, and, having no alternative other than to compete against men, she did so on an equal basis. Her feeling for horses caused her to convert the Pebble Hill dairy barns into stables and, later, to become an important breeder of thoroughbred horses.[5]

"She'd rather hear a pack of hounds running than eat when she was hungry." Such were the musings of Herbert Roundtree who was in charge of Pansy's hound kennels for fifty years. Possessed of a droll sense of humor, the black man recalled Mrs. Poe's fondness for her pack of Walker hounds. The pack was begun in 1934 when she purchased some registered foxhounds from S. L. Woolridge in Kentucky. In Thomas County and in Florida the hounds were used to hunt grey fox and wildcats. Usually, the hunts would begin before day and last until nine or ten in the morning. In the summer the pack would be taken to Kentucky where the owner had acquired property. There Arthur Massey, another longtime employee at Pebble Hill, hunted red fox with the Walkers. The larger red fox gave a longer, wider ranging chase than his grey kinsman, but both varieties, according to Roundtree and Massey, well deserve their reputation for cunning.[6]

Another intelligent forest animal, the raccoon, often tested "Miss Pansy's" abilities. When she was not coon hunting or pursuing fox and wildcats, the mistress of Pebble Hill might

---

[5]Author's interview with Parker Poe, April 10, 1979; *Thoroughbred Record*, December 27, 1978, 2388.

[6]Author's interview with Herbert Roundtree and Arthur Massey, April 12, 1979.

Elisabeth Ireland Poe
(1897-1978)
The gentle preserver of Pebble Hill.

well be hunting wild turkeys or ducks. She had a number of Yellow Labrador Retrievers that she used for duck hunting, although she also kept some Labs in her home as pets. The Welsh Corgi was another breed she liked, and for a time she owned several. Attracted by the challenge of shooting, she developed into a top shot. Commenting that Pansy "was good on quail," Roundtree added that she was "extra good on dove."[7]

Unlike many of her own free-wheeling outings, the hunts for guests were organized. Specially designed hunting wagons drawn by mules ranged the dirt roads that traversed the large acreage laid aside for the sport. Under close supervision the property was burned off at intervals to keep the woods free from dense undergrowth. Besides giving the birds and hunters more freedom of movement, controlled burning provided many ecological benefits. Such farming as occurred was the methodical laying out of fields and the planting of grain crops to feed the wildfowl.

The most casual encounter with the mistress of Pebble Hill left one with the sense of how important animals and the outdoors were to her. "I think horses and dogs was her life, or at least the biggest part of it," Clyde Bryant, her Stableman for twenty-five years, remarked a few months after she died.[8] Thelma Lawyer put it simply, "She loved animals."[9] In complete agreement was Herbert Roundtree. "Dogs and horses was her heart," he said. "I'm telling you what I know. If you want to get along with Miss Pansy treat her dogs good and horses, too." For emphasis he added, "That's the truth."[10]

---

[7]Author's interview with Herbert Roundtree, April 12, 1979.
[8]Author's interview with Clyde Bryant, April, 16, 1979.
[9]Author's interview with Thelma Lawyer, April 16, 1979.
[10]Author's interview with Herbert Roundtree, April 12, 1979.

"These Legs Don't Want Me"

During the war years of the 1940's Elisabeth Ireland was busy with her usual activities plus many patriotic endeavors. In 1942 she met Parker Poe. Born July 10, 1914, on his grandfather's ranch in Eastland County, Texas, Poe was, at the time, going through Officers' Candidate School at Fort Benning in Columbus, Georgia. Before going into the service he had graduated from the University of Texas (1934) and worked in New York in the Wall Street office of the Northern Pacific Railroad company. One weekend he visited Pebble Hill with Malcolm McBride, a fellow OCS candidate, native of Cleveland, and an old friend of the Harvey family. Parker and Pansy met again later and then corresponded after Poe was sent to the Pacific theatre of action. A heavy weapons company commander, he participated in the fighting on Leyte Island in the Philippines and Okinawa. Discharged as a major, Poe returned home and resumed the courtship.[11]

The wedding took place at Pebble Hill on the afternoon of April 5, 1946. The evening before the wedding Pansy's brother and his wife Margaret gave a fish fry for the couple at Ring Oak, their place in Florida. The wedding breakfast was given at Melrose by Fanny Mann Bolton (daughter of Howard Melville Hanna, Jr., and widow of Julian C. Bolton who died in 1942). Poe's mother, his sister, and her husband were present along with the bride's family and friends. Livingston gave the bride away, and Helen Matthews, secretary to both Kate Harvey and Pansy, was maid of honor. Bruce Lamb, Parker's brother-in-law, was best man. The ceremony was performed by Marshall Woodson, a Presbyterian minister.[12]

Mrs. Poe always strongly identified with her mother, carrying on many of Kate's projects and inaugurating num-

---

[11]Author's interview with Parker Poe, April 10, 1979.

[12]*Ibid.;* author's interview with Alice Massey, April 10, 1979; Thomasville *Times-Enterprise*, April 6, 12, 1946.

Robert Livingston Ireland, Jr., and Parker B. Poe

Arthur Massey and Herbert Roundtree, two longtime employees
at Pebble Hill, in 1979

erous one of her own. The women made tow annual events particularly important for the works on the plantation. One was the yearly Christmas tree party where the employees sang and staged pageants and received cash bonuses, The other was the celebration of Emancipation Day every May 20. On that day goats and hogs were barbecued, and the blacks celebrated their freedom with a savory feast and various activities.

In the 1940's Pansy bought Mayhaw plantation, approximately 4,440 acres, located in the eastern part of Thomas County; Dixie plantation, 2,200 acres in Brooks County; and land in Jefferson County, Florida, centered around Honey Lake where she built a boat house. The acreage at Pebble Hill with occasional exchanges of land remained at about 4,000 acres. After "Mr. Mac" died in 1946, he was succeeded by Neil C. Boland. A native of Camden County, Georgia, and educated at the state university, Boland remained as plantation manager until his death in 1976. There was no fulltime manager until Michael Singletary took over in 1978. Singletary, born in Thomas County, worked closely with Mrs. Poe in establishing future plans for the plantation. Richard St. John of Cleveland, Pansy's longtime financial advisor and friend, was intimately involved with the planning of the Pebble Hill Foundation.[13]

Given her love of horses, it seemed inevitable that Mrs. Poe would own land in Kentucky. In 1939, she bought 700 acres near Harrodsburg and developed Shawnee Farm. In the early 1940's Pansy bought 1,500 acres across the Kentucky River from Shawnee Farm in Jessamine County. She named it Fox Bend and used it mainly for fox hunting. After World War II she began breeding thoroughbreds at Shawnee and later, on a reduced scale, in Ireland. As a commercial breeding farm, Shawnee had its yearlings sold in the United States

---

[13]Author's interview with Michael Singletary, April 10, 1979.

and abroad. Pansy's interest in thoroughbreds and racing won her numerous honors including a special award in 1972 from the Thoroughbred Club of America.[14]

In 1951, Parker Poe purchased a home in Camden, Maine, where he and Pansy spent part of each year. Known as "The Rocks," the property was sold in 1978.

Mrs. Poe was fond of Appaloosas and quarterhorses, keeping them at Pebble Hill. Because she spent most of the year in Georgia, from November to the first half of July (as she grew older more and more time was spent at Pebble Hill), she brought her thoroughbred hunters with her. A ritual developed whereby the first week of July saw Stableman Clyde Bryant and others get the horses ready to go to Kentucky. Some three vans of them would be taken to the blue grass pastures of Shawnee farm, and the ritual would be reversed in the middle of November when the animals were brought back to Thomas County. In the spring of 1979 Bryant remembered how closely his employer looked after the whole process of safely moving the horses. "She was a great lady in my book," he recalled with nostalgia. "It's kinda hard to get adjusted to the way things are now without her."[15]

People who knew her never ceased to be amazed at Mrs. Poe's energy or the breadth of her interests. Short in stature, hardly over five feet tall, and heavy as she got older, Pansy disdained fancy clothes and, for that matter, fancy talk. Never one to suffer fools, she was highly intelligent, cutting to the heart of any topic at issue, and fiercely loyal. Plantation manager Singletary remarked that "She had more

---

[14]*Thoroughbred Record*, December 27, 1978, 2388. Mrs. Poe was also the first woman named to the board directors of the Keeneland Association (1955); in 1958 she received the ladies sportsmanship award presented annually by the Kentucky Thoroughbred Breeders Association.

[15]Author's interview with Clyde Bryant, April 16, 1979.

145

A Pebble Hill road flanked by magnolia trees

interests than she had time." He thought the woman's outstanding quality was "her amazing interest in so many diverse subjects."[16] Noting his wife's major collections, Parker Poe mentioned arrowheads; milk glass animals; American pressed glass with animals; scrimshaw (tusks of walruses and sea animals carved and then inked); horse bronzes (among them a full set of work by Tex Wheeler); Royal Copenhagen porcelain, largely animals; stamps; coins; sporting pictures, especially Audubon bird prints; horn carvings; porcelain, Chinese export eighteenth century; and books—a good sporting library devoted to hounds, horses, and birds. Her brother agreed that Pansy "was an inveterate collector."[17]

Mrs. Poe was shy in the presence of crowds, but she had an Irish wit and temper. She was not totally unfamiliar with profanity, but when displeased she usually would peer over her glasses, go through a series of rapid head inclinations toward each shoulder and denounce as "gol-durned" whatever had raised her ire. What mattered to her was preserving the beauty of Thomasville and Thomas County, and she led numerous battles to keep trees from being cut down, restore historic homes, and prevent the needless widening of streets. She often wondered aloud—in one of her favorite expressions— what was going to happen, "When I kick the bucket."

She was appalled at disorder and waste and wanted things done properly. Thelma Lawyer mentioned that Pansy "believed you've got to do your job good," and that while she liked to tease, the signal for seriousness was her eyes: "Those eyes just would not be still." Her employer might get angry, but she never condescended. "To me," Mrs. Lawyer remembered, "Miss Pansy was just an ordinary, common person," one

---

[16]Author's interview with Michael Singletary, April 16, 1979.

[17]Author's interview with Parker Poe, April 10, 1979. Author's interview with Robert Livingston Ireland, Jr., May 15, 1979.

whose attitude was "your trouble is my trouble."[18] Thrifty, saving, opposed to waste—such were the qualities Glen Sanford saw in Mrs. Poe. Having worked for her at Pebble Hill for many years, Sanford agreed that "She wasn't a fancy person at all." She required performance, but she was also patient. "If you asked her a question she'd take time to answer your question and see that you saw into it."[19]

As an extremely private person, Mrs. Poe kept most of her donations and charities quiet or anonymous. She was a longtime member of the Thomas County Historical Society and of Thomasville Landmarks, Inc. Largely responsible for building the Thomasville Garden Center, she also bought, improved, and donated the property on which the town's historic "Big Oak" was situated. She purchased a gazebo and had it placed on the lot where the giant liveoak stands. She helped organize the Thomas County Humane Society; contributed to Tall Timbers Research, an environmental organization; and for thirty-three years was a trustee of Thomasville's Archbold Memorial Hospital. At Harrodsburg she was a board member of the James B. Haggin Memorial Hospital and of the Mercer County Humane Society. She deeded her Fox Bend Farm to Shakertown and served on the board of trustees of Shakertown at Pleasant Hill, Inc. To those agencies and institutions, as well as many others, she gave her time, energy, and financial support.

Like her mother, Mrs. Poe had a wide range of friends, and like her mother, she always had a large guest list at Pebble Hill. Notables ranging from President Dwight D. Eisenhower to the Duke and Duchess of Windsor visited the plantation. They, no less and no more, received and were impressed by the simple dignity and courtesy that Pansy offered to people.

---

[18]Author's interview with Thelma Lawyer, April 16, 1979.
[19]Author's interview with Glen Sanford, April 16, 1979.

While governor of Georgia, Jimmy Carter, in Thomasville for a dedication service, visited Pebble Hill. He had his picture taken with the owner and inscribed the photograph: "With love to Pansy Poe, one of the finest women I know." No doubt she was flattered by the future President's sentiments, but Pansy would have been more pleased by Thelma Lawyer's appraisal: "She liked you for what you are," or Glen Sanford's that "You can't beat her. She always tried to help you out."[20] Loyalty is another measure of esteem. Mrs. Mary Ann Mitchell began working for Kate Ireland during Theodore Roosevelt's administration and later transferred her employment to Pansy. Mrs. Mitchell retired during the Presidency of Gerald Ford— a tenure of seventy-two years. In 1979 she was living at Pebble Hill and was 103 years old.

Parker Poe pointed out that his wife had an abiding sense of humor and, like her mother, a profound love for Pebble Hill. She had as well a sense of history. Married later in life, the Poes had no children. Although numerous relatives continued to own land in Thomas County, they were busy with their own interests. Believing that the public would be interested in visiting the main house, grounds, stables, garages, and various buildings of a historic plantation, Mrs. Poe created the Pebble Hill Foundation. That private organization maintains the plantation as it is today.

In the late fall of 1978 Mrs. Poe returned to Pebble Hill from Kentucky. Obviously tired, she attempted to continue her frenetic pace, but early in December she suffered a heart attack. It was characteristic that on being taken to the hospital in an ambulance, she removed the oxygen breathing mask, insisting she could manage better without it; she then gave word that the siren and flashing red light were to be turned

---

[20]Author's interviews with Thelma Lawyer and Glen Sanford, April 16, 1979. See also Harrodsburg [*Kentucky*] *Herald*, December 21, 1978.

off, and ordered the driver to slow down. For a time she seemed to recover.

On Saturday morning, December 16, Alice Massey, Pansy's close friend and personal maid, gave her a bath at 11:30 and fixed her hair. Al Cofield, manager of Shawnee Farm, was due to arrive in the afternoon. The two women sat and talked about Christmas. Alice was given the responsibility for giving out the presents. Before the black woman departed she helped Mrs. Poe with her crutches when she entered an adjoining room in preparation for Cofield's visit. Having difficulty walking, Pansy said to Alice, "These legs don't want me." Alice assured her that they did. Mrs. Massey soon heard heavy breathing and entered the room in time to cradle Pansy's head as she died quietly. It was ten minutes past twelve o'clock.[21]

Mrs. Poe was buried in the cemetery at Pebble Hill. The private ceremony was limited to her husband and members of the immediate family. Later, the employees on the plantation held a moving memorial service at the Piney Grove Baptist church, which she had earlier built for them. There was also a memorial service at Thomasville's St. Thomas Episcopal church.

What Thomas Jefferson Johnson had wrought from a wilderness, John W. H. Mitchell and Julia Ann had continued. Then, in turn, Kate Harvey and Pansy Poe had enlarged the plantation and made the systematic care, preservation, and perpetuation of woods, wildlife, and land central to Pebble Hill. What is meaningful in one's life varies with the individual. What Elisabeth Ireland Poe remembered enjoying was "going on long trips with a four in hand and coming home at all

---

[21]Author's interview with Alice Massey, April 10, 1979. See also Thomasville *Times-Enterprise*, December 18, 1978; Thomasville *Courier*, December 21, 1978.

hours singing our heads off—Then coon hunting with fat wood torches & the mule wagon rides home—singing the old spirituals with the colored men—going on many a picnic for the shooting guests, canoeing down the river—Riding & driving on the grand plantation roads."[22]

---

[22]Recollections of Mrs. Parker Poe.

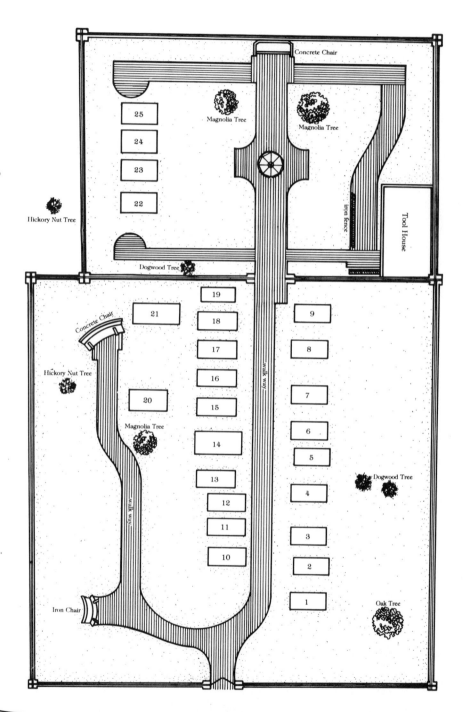

Family Cemetery

APPENDIX

PERSONS BURIED IN PEBBLE HILL CEMETERY

1 Ewen MacLean
Died on the 12th February, 1855
In the 49th year of his age

2 Kenneth MacLean
Died on the 15th March, 1842
In the 23rd year of his age

3 James Decatur Thomas
Born December 24th, 1815
Died August 19th, 1841
Aged 25 yrs., 7 mos. & 25 days.

4 Nellie Johnson Everett

5 Barbara Johnson
wife of
Richard H. Thomas
Born May 18th, 1788
Died Jan. 9th, 1862

6 James Johnson
Born 1753
Died Dec. 3rd, 1833

7 Jane W. Hadley
wife of
Thomas Jefferson Johnson
Born Nov. 15th, 1798
Died Sept. 22nd, 1830

8 Jane Martha Johnson
Born March 27th, 1828
Died Aug. 17th, 1842

9 Simon D. Hadley
Brother of Jane Hadley Johnson
and of Samuel Hadley

10 Dr. William P. Holland

11 Richard James MacLean
Capt. Co. E, 50th Ga. Vol. Inf.
Killed, Battle of Salem Church,
May 3rd, 1863: age 21 yrs.

12 John Ewen MacLean
Sgt., Co. E, 29th Ga. Vol. Inf.
"Ochlockonee Light Inf." Died
Sept. 17th, 1865

13 Julia Anne Johnson
wife of
John William Henry Mitchell
Born June 7th, 1829
Died Jan. 21, 1881

14 John William Henry Mitchell
Born April 8th, 1828
Died March 5th, 1865

15 Nathaniel Raines Mitchell
Born Dec. 13th, 1854
Died March 5th, 1865

16 Thomas Jefferson Johnson
Born Jan. 17th, 1793
Died Nov. 6th, 1847

17 Martha J. Evans
Second wife of
Thomas Jefferson Johnson
Died, March, 1850

18 Lucy Hill
Second wife of
Nathaniel Raines Mitchell

19 Infant son of
Dr. & Mrs. Robert J. Bruce

20 Robert Goodwin Wheeler
son of Richard Wheeler
Born March 31st, 1868
Died April, 1888

21 Duncan Ray, Sr.

22 Perry Williams Harvey
Born May 10th, 1869
Died May 24th, 1932

Son of Henry Allyn and Mary
Williams Harvey

23 Kate Hanna Harvey
Born Dec. 26th, 1871
Died May 15th, 1936
Daughter of Howard Melville
and Kate Smith Hanna

24 Elisabeth Ireland Poe
31 X 1897—16 XII 1978

25 Marker for Parker Barrington
Poe 10 VII 1914—

BIBLIOGRAPHY

PRIMARY SOURCES

Federal and State Records, Published and Typescript
Acts of Georgia, 1823, 1825-1826, 1831, 1835, 1837-1838, 1905.
Adjutant General's Letter Book (typescript), 24, April 29-June 3, 1864, Georgia Department of Archives and History (GDAH), Atlanta.
American State Papers, Indian Affairs, II. Washington: Gales and Seaton, 1834.
Bennett, Hugh H., and Mann, Charles J., "Soil Survey of Thomas County Georgia," *Field Operation of the Bureau of Soils*. N. P.: N. P., N.D.
Bryan, Mary Givens (Compiler), *Georgia Official and Statistical Register, 1957-1958*. Hapeville: Longino & Porter, 1958.
Catalogue of the Trustees, Officers and Alumni of the University of Georgia from 1785-1894. Atlanta: Foote & Davis, 1894.
Creek Indian Letters Talks And Treaties, 4 parts, taken from original manuscripts as a Works Progress Administration (WPA) project, GDAH.
Final Report of the United States DeSoto Expedition Commission. Washington: Government Printing Office, 1939.
Hayes, Mrs. J. E. (Arranger), *Georgia Military Affairs*, III (1801-1813), IV (1814-1819), V (1820-1829) in GDAH.
Hayes, Mrs. J. E. (Arranger), *Georgia Military Record Book 1778-1839* in GDAH.
Lamar, Lucius Q. C., *A Compilation of the Laws of the State of Georgia . . . Since The Year 1810 to the Year 1819 . . .* Augusta: T. S. Hannon, 1821.
Prosperous Georgia The Ideal Home For All Classes. Bulletin Georgia Department of Agriculture Serial No. 52-B. Atlanta: N. P., 1910.
Thomas County File, GDAH.
White, George, *Statistics of the State of Georgia*, Savannah.

Manuscripts And County Records

Decatur County

Deed Record Book A, B, E. Circuit Clerk's Office, Decatur County Courthouse, Bainbridge, Georgia.

Grady County

Bond for Title, Book I. Circuit Clerk's Office, Grady County Courthouse, Cairo, Georgia.
Deed Record Book 10, 25, 27, 31, 36, 43, 66. Circuit Clerk's Office, Grady County Courthouse.

Pulaski County

Deed Record Book E. Circuit Clerk's Office Pulaski County Courthouse, Hawkinsville, Georgia.

155

Thomas County

Circuit Clerk's Office

Book D, 1844, Superior Court Records.
Book E, 1845, Superior Court Records.
Declaration Book B, Superior Court Records.
Deed Record Book A, B, C, D, E, F, G, H, I, L, O, P, Q, R, S, T, U,
    V, X Y, AA, BB, DD, EE, FF, GG, II, JJ, KK, LL, MM, NN,
    OO, PP, RR, TT, WW, XX, ZZ, A-1, A-M, D-2, 3-C, 3-E, 3-S,
    3-T, 4-A, 5-G.
Mortgage Record Book J, M, E-M, H-M, I-M.
Writ Record, 1842-1848, Book H.

Ordinary's Office (Judge of Probate)

Book 2, 1837-1849.
Book 3, 1849-1854.
Book E, 1849-1852.
Book 4, 1854-1860.
Book U.
Bond Book 1849-1859, E; 1880-1913, I.
Court Docket 1854-1868, H.
General Book B, 1837-1843.
Inventory and Appraisement, F, 1847 To 1867.
Letters of Administration, Book J.
Oaths Book.
Marriage Record 1826-1837, Book A; 1836-1865, Book B; 1856-1881, Book
    H; 1885-1889, Book K; 1915-1928, Book L.
Minutes, 1856-1860, H; 1860-188?, X.
Returns 1845-1849; 1875-1877; Book D, D-1, D-2.
Tax Digest, 1890, 1891, 1893, 1894, 1895, 1896, 1897, 1898, 1899, 1900.
Will Book 1850-1855; 1915-1928, Book L.

Special Collections

Hitz, Alexander M., compilation. This is a carefully assembled list of
    people who received land in Thomas County in Georgia's 1820 land
    lottery. It also contains information concerning the 1827 and 1832
    lotteries.
Hopkins, Elizabeth F., collection. An extensive and invaluable assembly
    of materials relating to Thomas County, especially families. It is
    the property of the Thomas County Historical Society.
King, Thomas Butler, papers, GDAH.
Mitchell, J. W. H., "Sketch of Pebble Hill." The manuscript is the prop-
    erty of the Thomas County Historical Society.
Mitchell, Nathaniel Raines, papers, GDAH.
Recollections of Mrs. Parker Poe. These notes were written in pencil
    in the last fall of 1978. They are the property of Parker Poe of
    Thomasville.

156

Bibliography

Thomasville United Daughters of the Confederacy Historical Collection IV, 1932. Copy in the Thomas County Historical Society Collection.

Newspapers And Magazines

Augusta *Centennial Chronicle*, 1885.
Butler [Alabama] *Choctaw Herald*, 1875.
Harrodsburg [*Kentucky*] *Herald*, 1978.
Macon *Georgia Messenger*, 1825.
New York *Times*, 1928.
Savannah *Georgian*, 1825, 1836.
Tallahassee *Floridian*, 1836.
Thomasville *Courier*, 1978.
Thomasville *Press*, 1930.
Thomasville *Semi-Weekly Times-Enterprise*, 1921, 1923, 1936.
Thomasville *Southern Enterprise*, 1860, 1861, 1865, 1866.
Thomasville *Weekly Times-Enterprise*, 1893.
Thomasville *Wiregrass Reporter*, 1860.
Thoroughbred Record [Lexington, Kentucky], December 27, 1978, 2388.

Interviews

Throughout the book specific citations are given to interviews. Over a period of nineteen years Mrs. Parker Poe was a constant source of information. Useful interviews were permitted by the following citizens of Thomasville: Louise Boland, Gertrude Haskell Britton, Clyde Bryant, Robert Livingston Ireland, Jr., Thelma Lawyer, Alice Massey, Arthur Massey, Parker Poe, Herbert Roundtree, Glen Sanford, Michael Singletary, and Polly Singletary.

Primary And Secondary Books And Articles

Georgia

Balfour, R. C., Jr., *The History of St. Thomas Episcopal Church.* Tallahassee: Rose Printing Company, 1968.

Bolton, Herbert E., and Ross, Mary, *The Debatable Land, A Sketch Of the Anglo-Spanish Contest for the Georgia Country.* Berkeley: University of California Press, 1925.

Bryan, T. Conn, *Confederate Georgia.* Athens: University of Georgia Press, 1948.

Callaway, James Ethridge, *The Early Settlement of Georgia.* Athens: University of Georgia Press, 1948.

Chappell, J. Harris, *Georgia History Stories.* New York: Silver, Burdett, and Company, 1905.

Clements, J. B., *History of Irwin County.* Atlanta: N. P., 1932.

Coulter, E. Merton, *A Short History of Georgia.* Chapel Hill: University of North Carolina Press, 1933.

General James Jackson Chapter, D.A.R., *History of Lowndes County, Georgia, 1825-1941.* Valdosta: N. P., 1941.

Harper, Roland H., "Development of Agriculture in Lower Georgia 1850 to 1860," *Georgia Historical Quarterly*, VI (June, 1922), 97-121.

Pebble Hill: The Story of a Plantation

Harris, Mrs. Wallace Leigh (Virginia Speer) (Compiler), *History of Puloski And Bleckey Counties, Georgia 1808-1956*, 2 vols. Macon: J. W. Burke Company, 1957 and 1958.

Hawkinsville Chapter Daughters of the American Revolution, *History of Pulaski County, Georgia*. Atlanta: Walter W. Brown, 1935.

Howell, Clark, *History of Georgia*, 4 vols. Chicago-Atlanta: S. J. Clarke Publishing Co., 1926.

Huxford, Folks, *The History of Brooks County, Georgia*. Athens: McGregor Company, 1949.

Jones, Frank S., *History of Decatur County, Georgia*. Atlanta: N. P., 1971.

Lanning, John Tate, *The Spanish Missions of Georgia*. Chapel Hill: University of North Carolina Press, 1935.

Le Conte, Emma, *When The World Ended The Diary of Emma Le Conte* (edited by Earl Schenck Miers). New York: Oxford University Press, 1957.

Le Conte, Joseph, *'Ware Sherman A Journal of Three Months' Personal Experience in the Last Days of the Confederacy*. Berkeley: University of California Press, 1937.

McCallie, S. W., *Phosphates and Marls of Georgia*. Atlanta: N. P., 1896.

MacIntyre, W. Irwin, *History of Thomas County, Georgia*. Thomasville: N. P., 1923.

Miller, Stephen F., *The Bench And Bar Of Georgia Memoirs And Sketches*, 2 vols. Philadelphia: L. P. Lippincott, 1858.

Myers, Robert Marson (Editor), *The Children of Pride A True Story of Georgia And The Civil War*. New Haven: Yale University Press, 1972.

Pond, Cornelia Jones, *Life On A Liberty County Plantation. The Journal Of Cornelia Jones Pond* (edited by Josephine Bacon Martin). Darien: N. P. 1974.

Rogers, William Warren, *Ante-Bellum Thomas County 1825-1861*. Tallahassee: Florida State University Press, 1963.

Rogers, William Warren, *Thomas County During The Civil War*. Tallahassee: Florida State University Press, 1963.

Rogers, William Warren, *Thomas County 1865—1900*. Tallahassee: Florida State University Press, 1973.

Shelton, Jane Twitty, *Pines And Pioneers A History Of Lowndes County, Georgia 1825-1900*. Atlanta: Cherokee Publishing Company, 1967.

Smith, George Gillman, *The Story of Georgia and the Georgia People 1733 to 1860*. Macon: Franklin Company, 1900.

Steel, Edward M., Jr., *Thomas Butler King of Georgia*. Athens: University of Georgia Press, 1964.

General

A Brief Biography Of Perry Williams Harvey. Cleveland: Horace Carr Printing Press, 1936.

Cotterill, [Robert] S., *The Southern Indians, The Story of the Civilized Tribes Before Removal*. Norman: University of Oklahoma Press, 1954.

Bibliography

Crane, Verner W., *The Southern Frontier 1670-1732*. Durham: Duke University Press, 1928.

Croly, Herbert, *Marcus Alonzo Hanna His Life And Work*. New York: MacMillan Company, 1923.

Dangerfield, George, *The Era of Good Feelings*. New York: Harcourt, Brace and Company, 1952.

Hamilton, Peter J., *Colonial Mobile*. Boston and New York: Houghton, Mifflin, 1898.

Hanna, Kathryn Abbey, *Florida Land of Change*. Chapel Hill: University of North Carolina Press, 1941.

Mahon, John K., *The War of 1812*. Gainesville: University of Florida Press, 1972.

Paisley, Clifton, *From Cotton To Quail An Agricultural Chronicle of Leon County, Florida 1860-1967*. Gainesville: University of Florida Press, 1968.

Rice, Charles Elmer, *A History of the Hanna Family* . . . Damascus: Aden Pim & Sons, 1903.

The Book Of Benjamin Hanna His Children And Their Descendants. Cleveland: Horace Carr Press, 1936.

Tucker, Glenn, *Tecumseh Vision of Glory*. New York: Bobbs-Merrill, 1956.

Wallace, David Duncan, *South Carolina A Short History*. Chapel Hill: University of North Carolina Press, 1951.

Wright, J. Lietch, Jr., *Anglo-Spanish Rivalry in North America*. Athens: University of Georgia Press, 1971.

Who's Who In America, XVIII. Chicago: A. N. Marquis Company, 1934.

INDEX

Index